MAD
ABOUT
THE
HOUSE

First published in the United Kingdom in 2020 by
Pavilion
43 Great Ormond Street
London
WC1N 3HZ

Illustration and design by Abi Read.

ISBN 978-1-91162-492-9

A CIP catalogue record for this book is available from the British Library.

10 9 8 7 6 5 4 3 2 1

Reproduction by Rival Colour Limited, UK
Printed and bound by 1010 Printing International Ltd., China

www.pavilionbooks.com

MAD ABOUT THE HOUSE

101 Interior Design Answers

KATE WATSON-SMYTH

PAVILION

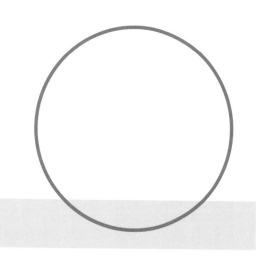

CONTENTS

Your Home, Your Story   6
   A Word About Trends &
      a Thought on Sustainability   8
   The Six Questions You Need to Ask   13

Layout & Flooring   27
Painting & Decorating   63
Windows & Doors   89
Fixtures & Furnishings   103
Lighting   121
Cooking & Dining   137
Lounging & Working   155
Bathing & Sleeping   173

Top Tips for Renters
   & First-time Buyers   191

Resources   194
Index   196
Acknowledgements   200

YOUR HOME, YOUR STORY

I have been writing about interiors for 20 years and helping clients to style their homes for more than 10. A couple of years ago I went to meet a client to help her with the finishing touches to her home...

I was there for nearly three hours looking at all the rooms, seeing what she had already done and where she still needed help or ideas. We discussed how she was using each space and what was missing. Then I drew up a report covering everything we had talked about and included photos for inspiration and links to items we had decided she might need, with several options for each piece. A couple of weeks later I received an email from her. The consultation, she wrote, had been 'quite' helpful. She knew what she now needed and was making plans to get hold of it all. But she couldn't help pointing out that she was also a little disappointed.

My stomach flipped over. 'I don't know what my style is so I don't feel completely happy with the service,' she said. My stomach flipped back. I stared thoughtfully out of the window for a few moments. 'Your style,' I typed firmly, 'is modern rustic.' A few minutes later my inbox pinged: 'Thank you so much. It's been so helpful to meet you and I'm so excited to finish off all the details of the house. I would thoroughly recommend you to anyone.' And after reading that I couldn't help but wonder (cue Sex and the City voice-over), do we all need to belong to a gang to feel valid? Do we need to find our interior design squad before we can be really happy in the space we have created?

Now I would say no. Emphatically not. Probably… However, it is true that in these days of online shopping it definitely helps if you can attach a label to your style so that you can hunt down what you want out there on the big old internet. Are you looking for a shabby-chic dressing table, or a modern rustic kitchen table? Is your living room country casual or urban glamour? I have wasted many an hour searching for a thingumajig only to find them in plentiful supply once I realized that what I actually needed was a thinguma*bob*. So yes, you do need to know your style so you can find your tribe. Or at least your sofa.

It's a topic I dealt with at length in my last book, and while this is intended as a more practical guide, it's worth recapping for those of you who have arrived here first. Knowing your style means that you can buy less, because you will buy well. Knowing your style will save you money, because you won't be making mistakes. And it means – and this relates to another question I am asked on a weekly basis – that your home will have an automatically cohesive look, because you will be shopping from the same palette and style and everything will fit together. (Which is not to say you can't fling a neon cushion into a room full of pastels, but do that in more than one place or it might look a bit random.)

Once you have worked out your style and feel comfortable with everything you have chosen, then your home will automatically tell the story of the people who live within its walls. It will have a more considered appearance, which might sound like posh interior design talk, but actually just means that it will look like you thought about it and made a decision about what you were buying.

One of the most welcoming things about a house is being able to get a sense of who it belongs to as soon as you walk inside. But does knowing your style and making the choice to stick to it mean you can never indulge in a spot of spontaneous trend shopping? Read on…

A WORD ABOUT
TRENDS
&

A THOUGHT ON
SUSTAINABILITY

This is a question I am asked more than any other: should I follow trends? The short answer is no, probably not, because you should buy only things you love and that you will love forever.

But the longer answer is that most of us do buy into trends (pun intended) to a certain degree, not least because they dictate what is available at any given time. Who hasn't tried to buy a navy sweater when all around is a sea of grey and black? Who hasn't noticed that the high-street windows all seem to have the same colours in them? (And woe betide you if you want something different.)

Contrary to what you might think, interior trends move much more slowly than fashion does. It starts on the pages of the magazines, then a few early adopters (usually interior designers and the so-called Instagram influencers) will bring it into their homes and show it off on social media. Bear in mind that this is partly because they will have seen it way before anyone else. Gradually it makes its way off the printed and digital page and into the home of someone you know. And so it begins.

What you see in Milan might not come to Milton Keynes for three years, but come it will.

Kimberly Duran, who blogs at Swoon Worthy, likens the rise and fall of trends to a bell curve, which she bases on E.M. Rogers' Diffusion of Innovation Theory (well yes, quite). What that means, she says, is that designers, innovators and trendsetters (about 2.5 per cent of the population) will be the first to use a specific material, colour or finish. It will then be embraced by early adopters (13.5 per cent).

There are two groups which make up the bulk of the population – in fact, around 68 per cent of people will fall into these categories. The first, the 'early majority', will adopt the trend when it begins to become more mainstream. Maybe they see their favourite bloggers post about it or they see it take off on Instagram. Once the trend hits its peak, you'll see it adopted by what is called the 'late majority'. These are the people who are now seeing it everywhere (from Pinterest to their local supermarket) and decide it's time to invest.

At the very tail end of the curve are the 'laggards' (16 per cent), for whom trends are mostly ignored, and so it's only once the trend has completely saturated the market and prices begin to fall that they will consider buying. This is important to know because how much time elapses from the beginning of the curve to the end (ie the full lifetime of a trend) varies considerably. Normally, Kimberly notes, the faster a trend reaches its peak the faster it will fall out of favour. At the same time, the longer a trend takes to be adopted by the majority, the longer it takes to fall out of fashion.

Don't forget that if stores see something selling well they are going to stock more of it, not less. That's why you may hear someone proclaim Millennial Pink is 'out' when in fact it has simply hit its peak and is now moving down the other side of the curve. You'll still find it in stores and you'll still see people buying up blush pink items. It's not really 'out' at all. It's just those early adopters – like the magazines and Instagrammers – have found something else to get excited about. And so it begins again with something different.

This bell curve also explains why copper, the trend that wouldn't die, was around for about six years. The early adopters and even the early majority had moved on about three

times before the laggards caught up. And then, of course, it had a second life when it was renamed 'rose gold' and everyone went mad for it all over again.

But woven through all this is the question of sustainability and the perils of throwaway culture. These days it just doesn't feel right to keep buying more and more stuff. Surely it's about making the right choices and living with them because we love them, rather than chucking things out after a year because someone tells us they're no longer on trend?

Well yes, but that doesn't mean we can't change things around. I have a box of summer clothes that I tend to only wear for two weeks of the year at the beach. Many of them are 10 years old and while I might add to them before each holiday – often buying in off-season sales – they tend to last for years because I know my style and I don't wear them that often. You can do the same thing with interiors. For example, changing the cushions with the seasons means you get to refresh and change the look of the room, but you don't have to chuck everything out and start again.

It's very hard to be sustainable in all our choices but we can start by being more aware and making small changes. I have three sofas – one I bought new,

one which belonged to my great grandmother and which has been reupholstered three times to my knowledge, and one I bought for my husband for his 40th birthday from a junk shop, which we have also reupholstered. That's two items which have been saved from landfill and which bring their own individuality and character to our home.

We can't all get it all right all of the time, but we can all be more aware. It's still possible to have fun but think about where your purchases are coming from. H&M, a global fashion brand that also sells homewares, aims to have 100 per cent sustainably sourced cotton in all ranges – including

home – from 2020. The rest of the high street will surely follow suit.

So it's not about ignoring trends; it's about feeling confident enough in your style and choices that you can buy into them when it's right for you and not panic if you are ignoring them. I wrote about how to find your style in the last book – in short, start by looking at the colours and shapes in your wardrobe and consider dressing your house like you dress yourself. But even if you know what you like and barely put a foot wrong when it comes to a flamingo cushion or a leopard print lampshade, it's still possible to examine your choices a little more closely, as we shall see.

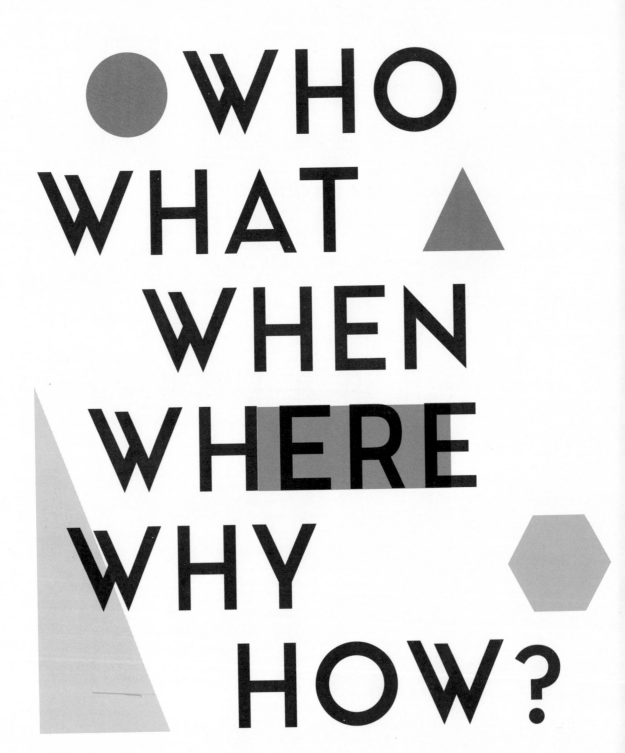

THE SIX QUESTIONS
YOU NEED TO ASK

I am constantly amazed by the number of people who just decorate a room the way they fancy. Of course, that is how it *should* look by the end of the process: a collection of objects, furniture and colours that so completely reflect the people who live there, that it looks as if it all just happened naturally. But there are a few steps between that look and all the care that goes into achieving it.

It's the equivalent in sartorial terms to, 'What this old thing? Just threw it on!' It's that no-makeup makeup look which we all know involves far more effort than you would normally make. Giving a room an air of just-put-together effortlessness takes a lot of thought and planning and, well, effort... I'm afraid you can't just fill the space with all the things you want and expect it to come together perfectly unless you are a professional stylist, or have an extremely good eye – in which case, you should be a professional stylist.

You need to plan it. All of it. But don't worry, that's not difficult if you know how – and I am going to tell you. It all comes down to six simple questions. That's it. It's that easy. Ask these questions before you start any interior design scheme, and you will not only create the room that is right for you, but also one that functions perfectly for your needs, feels like your home and makes your heart sing when you get back after a long day at work.

If you don't ask these questions (and more to the point, answer them honestly), you run the risk of ending up with a room that doesn't really work for the people who live there – which means they won't use it. Or, because there is no choice, they will use it, but it won't make them happy. And you will end up redecorating. Again.

So what are the six questions? Well here they are...

WHO, WHAT, WHEN, WHERE, WHY, AND HOW?

I trained as a journalist, not as a designer, and I began to realize that these six questions, which form the basis of any news story, are also the basis for any successful interior scheme. Actually, they work for pretty much anything. Even dinner. Who's coming? What do they want to eat? When are they arriving? Where will they sit? Why have they been invited? How will we cook it? And the chances are that you are already considering the answers.

Answer these questions first and everything will flow naturally. These answers will take you from lighting and colours to materials and accessories via furniture and the smaller decorative items. The form will follow from the function, but you need to think very carefully about the latter if you want the former to please you.

I know some people who spent a huge amount on a kitchen extension which was fitted out with all the latest high-tech equipment from a teppanyaki grill to a state-of-the-art range cooker. The reality of it was that neither of them particularly liked to cook and the room never quite acquired that happy state of homeliness that we all aspire to. Nor did it reflect the people who lived there so it never quite shed that showroom feel.

Using the Who, What, When, Where, Why, and How method will give you a road map to decorating your space and that means you will get the most use out of it. You will then be able to make plans for using every room in your house properly because each has a function or mode assigned to it. For instance, this is one of first questions I ask my clients when I visit: 'What are you doing in here?'

From there we might work out that one spot is perfect for morning coffee, another for early evening drinks, and another where the family might gather on a Saturday afternoon. Suddenly every place has a purpose and you have an idea of what to put in it. So, a Saturday morning coffee and papers area might work with two lively patterned armchairs or something with a more relaxed garden feel – rattan for example. A modular sofa lends itself to a family gathering, as opposed to a more formal sofa in a room that is for drinks and grown-ups, while the kids can go and jump on the saggy one in the playroom. So now that we know what the questions are, let's look at them in more depth. Remember:

Answer the questions, own the space.

I know it sounds simple, but how often do you actually think about this before you plan a room? I appreciate you know who lives in your house, but the requirements for a professional couple, a young family with small children, or a pair of retirees are all very different.

Take the kitchen for example. Is this a room for a cook or an eater? Knowing that will immediately determine the level of equipment and amount of work surface you need to plan for. For instance, if you're always in the kitchen at parties then you might want to dump the fancy oven for a wine fridge and throw in a few barstools.

This might be the moment to talk about honesty. Who is your real family? Because I'm going to hazard a guess it's not that lot off the TV who are bathed in perpetual sunshine as they float past each other – smiling and chatting about the day ahead while they make perfectly browned toast, never leave crumbs in the butter, and share intelligent thoughts about current affairs. Is the reality that mum's late and shouting, dad's pretending he's already left, teenagers are complaining about the lack of milk, the time, the weather, oh, and the cat's been sick in the corner...

If the latter is your truth, then by planning the room properly you have more chance of creating the former. I can't promise the teenagers will ever talk to you at 8am, but if you've done it right they'll come down for dinner – and they're quite often charming at that time of day.

What about the living room? Who exactly uses this space? A couple? Parents? A toddler and his toys? The teenagers and their mates? Does the whole family gather in there or is that an aspiration that has yet to be realized because the room wasn't planned according to anyone's needs? Answering these questions will help make that dream come true. Partly. The teenagers will probably never come out of their bedrooms for more than a quick grunt but you can at least create the right environment. Or plan enough storage for all the tat that invariably accompanies every toddler.

One final example? Who's in the bathroom? Is it used by an entire family who all need to get in and out in the morning in the most efficient time possible? Or will it be an en suite for adults who hanker after a spa experience? Perhaps it's for someone older who would quite like to replace the bath with a large walk-in shower that doesn't involve climbing in and out, because future proofing is always a good idea.

And, as you will see, getting the answers right on the *who* will help you make right decisions about the storage, which is often, in my experience, the single thing that people wish they had more of or wish they were able to rethink what they already have so it functions more efficiently.

So this is the first question you need to ask, because once you know *who* is using that room you can start to think about *what* they will be doing there.

This flows naturally from the first question, but it will force you to think in more detail about the kinds of things you will need to put in the room to make it work for the people who are going to be in there. The *what* answers the questions about the furniture and equipment that you need to get right if the *who* are going to use it properly.

Back to the kitchen. What are you doing? Will there be a lot of cooking? Because you will need to think about the type of oven required. Would a range cooker – which looks cool – fit into the available space you have? Or would an eye-level oven, which saves all that bending down to check if the cakes have risen, be better and kinder to the cook's back? And if this kitchen needs to cater for a large family, perhaps a five-burner hob would be better, but it will take up more space on the work surface. Gas is good, but induction is kinder to the planet. And it's worth noting that you should always buy the best appliances you can afford because, yes, you get what you pay for, and also it can help with resale values if that needs to happen as well.

Are small children going to be making their own breakfast? In which case you will need at least one low cupboard for bowls, spoons and simple food so that the dream of a very short lie-in at the weekend (with, admittedly, an avalanche of cereal to clean up afterwards) can be fulfilled. If your kitchen is the heart of the home and you fantasize of calmly preparing dinner while sipping wine as the children quietly do their homework at the table, then plan for that outcome. And when it doesn't quite work out that way you still get to drink the wine. You can create a space that fulfils all those desired functions if you have clearly worked out exactly what those functions are before you start.

'What are you doing?' is also a key question for the living room. Is it just a room for watching television? Is it for sipping drinks and chatting? Reading books or finding a quiet corner for a bit of life admin? Ask yourself: who will be in there and what will they be doing? That way you can work out if you need a comfy sofa with room for everyone to stretch out and watch films while eating popcorn, or if you need a smaller, more upright one which works for the occasional box set but is better for supporting a laptop. You can also start to make decisions about velvet versus linen and blinds versus curtains.

Put simply, knowing *what* you are doing helps with what you need to buy. And knowing what to buy will save you time, money and costly mistakes.

Having worked out *who* is going to be doing *what*, you arrive at the next question, which is: when? And with this question things start to get interesting, because it's about colour schemes and lighting.

So, when are you going to be doing it? I know the obvious answer is that you want to be able to do all of it, all of the time, but let's stop and think things through. The reality of my life is that by the time the boys have eaten, I've finished work, sorted out the laundry, my husband's back from work and we've had a glass of wine in the kitchen while preparing dinner, we never make it to the living room until about 9pm. So, *our* living room is definitely an evening room. And it's painted dark with ambient lighting. But *your* living room might double up as a home office. It might be where you have the dining table because the kitchen is small. It might also be the playroom. In short, it might need to work hard all day and cater for different age groups.

That means that however much you hanker after a dark and moody colour scheme, it might not be the right place, or time of life to do it. But you could think about a half-painted wall with a dark colour at the bottom. That will hide sticky finger marks and disguise the big black box that is the television.

And you can make the ceiling look higher if you paint it the same colour as the top half of the walls, thus blurring the edges and making the room appear bigger. If you have built-in storage, then paint it to match the walls so that it blends in and doesn't crowd the space. This will also make your shelves function as display units, as well as just storage.

Knowing when you are doing something is crucial to the final look of the room. Will you need a central pendant light to illuminate the whole space? Or is it about creating an inviting atmosphere with soft pools of illumination? While downlights in the kitchen will give you enough light to let you chop an onion, do you need something softer if it's where you will be eating dinner as well? Not least to hide the washing up till later. And don't forget something to create that spa feeling in the bathroom where low lighting is safer than candles and quicker to turn off.

If you are refurbishing a building, the electrician is going to want answers to the question of lighting well before the walls have been plastered so you will need to think about the *when* fairly early on in the scheme. Knowing *when* you will use a room is the key point to planning the whole look.

WHERE? Now, of course, you could simply dismiss this question as, 'Where are you decorating?' But I'm assuming if you've come this far that you've pretty much nailed that one. Consider instead, where will you be getting the things you need? Where are you going to shop? You will need to refer to the *how* for this as it will help with the question of budget, which will largely dictate the *where*.

If you've worked out that most of the money is going to the builder (as it did in our case) then you won't be popping down to Ann Sacks for bespoke tiles at £10 a pop, will you? Having said that, there are work-arounds. When we did our house up it was 2000–01, just as the UK VAT rate was about to increase from 17.5 per cent to 20 per cent. As a result, lots of companies were doing huge promotions offering VAT at the

old rate if you bought before a certain date. So we had a fridge wrapped up and sitting in a half-built room, along with a set of bifold doors that were four months away from being used. The point is, if you know you are doing a big project then wait for the sales. And these days, you can always ring up and ask if there are any deals about to come online. Companies will often offer you an extra discount if you ask.

You can also stagger your shopping to spread the costs, which means you may be able to spend the savings you make on the windows on some of those fancy tiles we spoke about. And talking of fancy tiles, you can always mix and match. We fell in love with some very expensive tiles for our bathroom but could only afford six of them. They were long and thin, so we just used them to make a low splashback behind each basin and stuck an Ikea mirror on the wall above to create the impression that it was all one piece (see opposite).

If you have your heart set on an expensive item from one shop, then stick that on the list and see where else you can go for the rest that might be cheaper. I have included advice throughout this book on where you can save and where you should really spend; for example, buy a good sofa because you don't want to be replacing that every couple of years, but spend less on lamps, which might be more trend driven. Plus, the key point of a lamp is the light it gives, not what the base is made from.

Another thing to consider is whether the item you have set your heart on exists in a more affordable version. I'm not suggesting you buy a copy or a knock-off, but you can often find items that were 'inspired by', or are 'similar to', and that can be a good way round a budgeting dilemma.

Thinking about where you shop also allows you to ponder the kind of shops you want to patronize. Is it about spending more but buying less from a domestic brand – maybe a small business – or do you need to go to larger companies that offer better prices and import from abroad? I'm not saying one is better than the other, I'm just saying that this is as good a time as any to think about it. We all have different ideas of what constitutes affordable, and there are times when the budget just won't allow us to shop for organic cotton. I don't say this to judge, merely to point out that there may come a time when you need to make a choice between craftsmanship and next-day delivery.

Put simply, 'Why are you doing this?' Because 'I want to add value' and 'I want to get more out of my home' are very different answers, with very different end results.

The estate agent may tell you not to remove the bath, but if you're a committed shower-taker with no plans to sell then you might want to ignore that advice in favour of what makes your home function better for you. Sometimes the outcome is the same. For example, converting the loft will undoubtedly add value as well as give you more space to live in, while built-in storage is 30 per cent more space efficient than freestanding.

Thinking hard about why you want to do something will also help you make the right design decisions. Why do you want a new kitchen? Because X, Y and Z are wrong with the current one, and once you have identified that you can think about how to put that right in a redesign. It is just as important to know what you don't want or like as what you do require and desire.

HOW? This is the practical one. You've worked out the *who*, *what*, *when*, *where* and *why*. You know what you want to do and how to make it fit your style and suit the people you live with. How, then, are you going to pay for it? You need to plan a budget – and to do that you need to prepare a scope of work.

Start by making a list of everything that needs doing. And don't think you can put off paying for new windows by spending the money on a new sofa – the sofa will be ruined by rain coming in from the leaking panes so you'll have to buy another one anyway. Try to think of every element of each job. We were once badly stung by a less-than-scrupulous builder who quoted for tiling a floor and then charged us extra for taking off all the doors and planing them to make sure they would still open, as the floor was now a few centimetres higher. We had assumed that this would have been accounted for in his quote. I think he 'forgot', and decided he could make more money. So, make the list and get the quote. And do ask if that will include extra details that may crop up.

Always have a contingency fund of around 10 per cent. A couple of years ago we decided to replace our garden decking with a cobblestone terrace. When the builder, who had quoted for this job, lifted the boards he discovered that the drain from the kitchen sink had been partially blocked for years and that coffee grounds and stuff from the sink that hadn't been able to go down the drain was piling up under the deck. For some reason it didn't smell until the decking was removed and then, boy, did it pong. So, we had to remove that smelly earth and pay for a new drain.

By the way, ask your builder if his quote includes materials. The usual practice is for them to add (with a mark-up of course) the cost of building materials such as sand and cement but for you to provide the paint yourself – if you want one of the labels, that is.

Budgeting may be boring, but it's vital I'm afraid. On pages 24 and 25 you'll find a checklist on how to plan a budget from Karen Knox – who has much better and more practical advice than I could ever hope to offer.

Based on @kim_dti

KAREN KNOX

CO-FOUNDER OF THE INTERIOR DESIGN COLLECTIVE

☐ Start with the bones and work outwards: There's no point painting over damp walls and hanging curtains over draughty windows. Those problems will only get worse over time, so you need to start with the problems first. Begin with the basics and then you can work up to the fun bits.

☐ The fireplace: Rather than agonizing over which picture to hang over it, you need to decide if you can live with the look of it. Do you need to replace the surround? Does the chimney work, or does it need relining? Would you ultimately prefer a wood-burning stove? The fireplace tends to be the focal point of the room. Get it right from the get-go.

☐ The windows: If they're ugly and draughty and need replacing then you need to do this first because replacing them will involve re-plastering the surrounding walls, and that will comprehensively mess up any existing décor. If they're uPVC and you can't afford to replace them, then you can paint them (see Q26), but it should still be one of the first jobs you consider.

☐ The radiators: A modern white panelled radiator is one of the ugliest things in a room. If you can't afford to replace, then repaint them – the same colour as the walls – so they disappear. If you have wallpaper, then pick one of the darkest, or strongest colours in the pattern and use that. Otherwise, are they in the right place? Radiators don't have to go under the window any more but that can often be the best place as they won't get in the way of your furniture. And if you want to resite them then floorboards will need to be raised to move the pipework, so you should do all that before you spend your money on sanding or carpet.

☐ The floorboards and walls: Boards will need a light sand if you are planning to leave them open with rugs on top. Walls in period homes often have layers and layers of wallpaper and paint on them. If you have woodchip, then deal with it at the start as it's a nightmare to cover over, and if it's on a ceiling, pulling it off may result in the need for a new plaster ceiling – which isn't just expensive, it's unbelievably messy.

- ☐ The lighting: Make sure switches and sockets are appropriate to the age of the house. There is masses of choice out there, and it's details like this that really make all the difference. If you're putting a pendant light on a ceiling, make sure it's a good one that draws attention for all the right reasons.

- ☐ The hall: This is the last place you should paint. It is, literally, the finishing touch. Because everything comes in and out through this space and it will be trashed by the end of any decorating project, so do it last.

- ☐ The bathroom: The first place you should decorate, because there's nothing worse when the whole house is covered in a thick layer of dust and you're cooking for four on a camping stove in the kitchen than not even having a nice place to get yourself clean. Do the bathroom first and then you can always go in there, lock the door and have a little cry. A clean one.

- ☐ Know where to compromise: The chances are that you have a certain amount of money in the pot and that's that. So you need to work out what you want versus what you can afford. Can you save money with some DIY? A smaller window? Fewer cupboards? Get three quotes from three builders and don't necessarily choose the cheapest. You generally get what you pay for (see Q8 for how to find the right tradespeople).

- ☐ Contingency fund: Ideally think in terms of 10 per cent of the overall spend. In a renovation project it's rare that you won't encounter something unexpected – like a ceiling that has to be replaced, or a drain moved, or brickwork needing repointing – and you will have to be able to pay for it somehow. And if by a miracle you don't need it, well there's always shoes…

NEXT QUESTION

So there you have the six big questions. Once you have answered them all honestly and in detail, you are ready to decorate your home. You should be able to avoid many of the most common mistakes and be able to create a space that works for the lifestyles of everyone under your roof.

But now I want to take a more practical look at all those details. After 10 million views and nearly 5 million visitors to the blog, I want to answer some of the most commonly asked questions that have cropped up over the years. Over the next eight chapters you will find the answers to all the essential issues, from which paint to use on the skirting boards, to how to zone an open-plan space, via the pros and cons of different kitchen work surfaces, and whether you could have a chandelier in your bathroom. I have looked at both big picture and small details, the windows, the walls, the flooring and the ceiling. Do you want curtains or blinds, a modular sofa or something vintage from Denmark? What sort of light bulb do you need and how bright should be it? How do you hang wallpaper, create a gallery wall or buy the right size rug? Or perhaps you want to know if underfloor heating is worth the expense, whether carpet is better than boards, or whether it's wise to remove the bath in favour of a large shower. I have addressed all these and many more in the coming pages, and I hope that if you have started with the first six big questions you will be able to create the home of your dreams.

LAYOUT & FLOORING

1

WHERE DO I START?

You have to start somewhere and I have learnt, through four house renovations, that the bathroom is the best room to begin with. If you are living on site during a big refurb, the dust and general dirt will end up being depressing. If you have a lovely bathroom where you can wash yourself (and let's be honest, probably the plates and pans as well), you will immediately feel better. Also, you can shut yourself in there and have a little cry when it all gets too much.

We only really worked this out in our current house, having previously always left the bathroom till last. Not only is living with a horrid bathroom depressing, but living with a horrid bathroom when you've got no kitchen is the pits. In our first flat we did the bathroom shortly before we moved out, when I was almost nine months pregnant. Having to lower myself to pee in a bucket in the corner of the bedroom and get myself up again with what turned out to be a 10lb baby in my body was one of the low points of my home renovations. So, bathroom first – you will thank me.

When it comes to where to start with an individual room, the sensible advice is that you should choose the colour for the walls last as that is the easiest thing to change. In practice, I find most people start there and try and bend things around it. However, there is usually a piece of furniture or a picture or something that you already have which is going to go in that room. Start there and build around that. A sofa will give you a jumping off point for the colours and style of the rest of the furniture. Sometimes it might be a piece of art, a postcard, or a scrap of material that has inspired you. Work out the starting point and then analyse what it is you like about that object. The colour? The style? The period? Don't forget how it makes you feel. Answering those questions will not only help you get started on the room décor but will also help you work out what to get rid of and what to keep in any given room.

For example, I had a client in a gorgeous 1930s house in the country who loved mid-century modern furniture. Now, you can mix the two together as, essentially, the clean lines of mid-mod will work with any period, but working out that this was the furniture she really liked meant that we were able to quickly conclude that the country-style radiator covers and ornate wall lights had to leave immediately. She didn't need my help to know that the curtains, with their tiebacks and pelmets, should be the second items out of the door. It was clear that her mid-mod Danish sofa, which needed reupholstering, was to be the starting point for the living room and everything flowed from there. The hand-painted coffee table with its floral design went to the bedroom and the nest of tables from eBay came in. The carved wooden chairs, with their ikat fabric, were sent out to the large hallway, while the vintage Parker Knoll came into the living room. By moving things around that she already owned we were able to instantly improve the space without spending any money.

So sometimes you'll find the answer lies not in the shops but in the other rooms of your house. They call it 'shopping your home', only it's free. Taking stock of all your furniture and moving it around allows you to fill the gaps in other rooms as well as providing a good starting point for the room you are working on. If you're in a position to provide most of the furniture from what you already have, then you can concentrate on the colours and patterns that you want to use.

2 HOW CAN A FLOOR PLAN HELP ME?

When you buy or rent a house you look at the floor plan to see how the rooms flow and how big they are. I find it's much easier to plan a space when I have a bird's eye view (as it were) rather than walking around and getting distracted by a sofa or pillar that I can't see round. I also find them very useful when thinking of moving internal walls to create new spaces.

If you are planning to move walls around then the floor plan will, roughly speaking, show you which are the supporting walls (thick black lines) and which are the stud walls (thin black lines). The supporting walls are holding the house up. They can be removed, but only if you have beams, or RSJs inserted to hold everything up. The size of the beam must be calculated by a structural engineer, who will work out the size and strength of the beam relative to how much house it is holding up. Usually the beams are then plastered over so they become part of the house's structure. Occasionally, if you are creating a very large opening, supporting pillars will be needed in the middle, at which point you have to work with them as an architectural feature. Removing walls like this obviously costs more than removing thin stud walls – which are much easier to knock through.

When it comes to listed houses, the rules are different and you may not be allowed to knock walls down. If you are buying a listed house, which may, for example, only have one bathroom, you might want to check the rules before you fill in the mortgage application. You usually need Listed Building Consent (or similar permission) from the planning authorities. Likewise, always check if the property is in a Conservation Area, as this will almost certainly have implications for changing the outside of a building with, for instance, a loft conversion. If you make an offer, your solicitor will deal with all that, but it's worth being aware of likely complications before you start spending any money on legal fees.

Sometimes a house is listed because it has interesting features – fireplaces, windows, etc – and you are not allowed to change them. Sometimes you won't be allowed to put a bathroom above a room with an important plasterwork ceiling below as leaks could damage it. Having said that, listing a building is not about freezing it in a period, it's just that you need to ask permission if you are planning to change any of the elements that gave it that status. The historic significance of a building is always, or should always, be weighed against its condition and function.

3 WHAT IS THE PURPOSE OF THE ROOM?

Just because someone is using a room as a bedroom doesn't mean that's what it has to be. There's a real reluctance to move rooms around from the traditional floor plan, and yet that layout may not work for you. You really need to think about your layout and how you will use the space.

We tend to put the kitchen at the back of the house with a view of the garden, which made sense when one had to stand at the sink washing up for ages. But now that we are taking down walls and creating open spaces it might be better to locate a sitting or dining area right at the back and stick the kitchen in the dark part towards the middle of the house. Yes, you will have to move some plumbing but the benefits of the way you can live in the space should outweigh that cost.

There's a reason that the Victorian front parlour was often small and that's because it was usually just for guests or Sundays, so it didn't need to be the biggest room. Think about how often you go in a room and what you are using it for.

I often see a home office crammed into the (second) smallest room in the house and then people wonder why they don't want to use it. I've done it myself – created a cramped office at the top of the house under the eaves. I banged my head every time I stood up. Unsurprisingly I spent six years working downstairs at the kitchen table. It's the same when it comes to the bedroom. Parents will often take the largest so-called master suite for themselves, but in fact they only go in there at bedtime and they don't have to store teepees, desks and playhouses in there – not to mention all the tiny trucks and dolls and general tchotchkes. In our last house we gave the biggest bedroom to our boys, with a set of bunk beds, and there was plenty of room for their toys, which meant the living room was a much tidier and more pleasant place to be.

If you are starting from scratch or thinking about adding an en suite, then consider making the bathroom a large and luxurious space. A big bathroom will always feel more 'hotel'. If possible, make space for a walk-in or through wardrobe (see Q98) and leave the smallest area for sleeping. After all – if you don't need to clutter it with clothes and storage, then all you need is space for the bed and a couple of side tables. The whole thing will be more Zen, so you will sleep better.

If you are buying a house then use the floor plan carefully to get an aerial view of the size and proportions of the rooms, and take note of the direction they face, to see if the right functions are in the right places.

The back of my house is north-facing and therefore frequently cold, while the living room – to the south – is often flooded with sunlight, which makes it a much nicer place to be on a winter's day. It's still seen as slightly odd to have the kitchen at the front of the house, but there's no doubt that we could have put the kitchen in the middle – or the back reception room of our Victorian house, and flipped the dining and living room from front to back, as I spend more time at the kitchen table than on the sofa. At least I should. And I would if there wasn't a delightful patch of sun that hits the sofa at about 3pm on a late winter's afternoon.

I'm not suggesting you turn the house upside down (although actually why not, if it would suit you better that way), but do at least have a think about how you use each room and if the current layout is right for you.

4

WHY YOU SHOULD
GO TO A HOTEL

Hotels are underrated as sources of inspiration. Think about it. The designers have to get a lot into a small space. There is usually one room – often not that big – which needs to house a bed, a table either side, a comfy chair or two, a desk, perhaps space for coffee- and tea-making, and clothes hanging. And then they've got to carve a luxurious bathroom out of a tiny corner.

It's always worth looking at hotel designs for their colour and materials choices. They are created by the people who often know not just what the next big things in terms of trends and colour schemes are likely to be, but are also expert at creating attractive, comfortable rooms in very uncompromising spaces.

So next time you're planning your summer holiday, don't just pay attention to the distance from the beach but take a look at the layout of the space, particularly the bathroom. In the Hoxton Hotel in Paris, the walls of the shower are frosted glass on two sides, which allows natural light from the bedroom to filter through to the bathroom (when did you ever see a hotel bathroom with a window?) but still allows for privacy. The door has a long horizontal handle, which serves not only its primary purpose but also to hang the towel or the bathmat when not in use.

Restaurant loos are another consistently good source of inspiration, not so much for space-saving tricks as for decorative ideas. Now, while I would never advise *you* to decorate for Instagram, there's no doubt that hotels and restaurants might do that. These days a good picture on the 'gram' is likely to result in a flood of bloggers and influencers turning up for a look. And that will lead to a flood of their followers visiting.

It's really not that unusual in some establishments to see one queue for the loo and another for the best photo-opp spot. Given that everyone will be buying a drink or a meal, it makes good business sense. The loo is a great place for a restaurateur to make a statement because it's comparatively small, so they can be daring with dramatic wallpaper, stunning tiles, spectacular sanitaryware, eye-catching glass, or a combination of all of these. And don't forget to look at the ceiling. While you're in there taking a picture for your grid, you might also be getting inspiration for your crib.

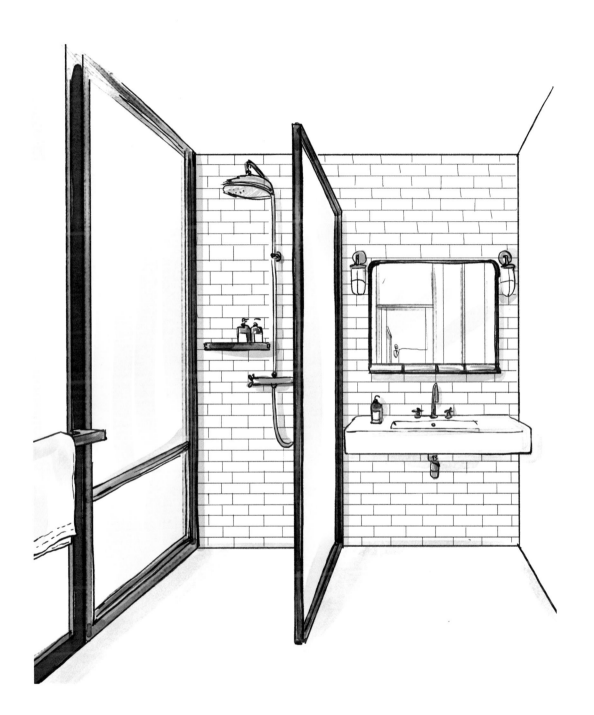

5 WHY YOU SHOULD MAKE A MOODBOARD

I wrote in the previous book about why Pinterest can be your frenemy – luring you down a rabbit hole of unsuitable ideas – and discussed how to make it work for you rather than against you, but there's no doubt that a collection of photographs showing what you want can be a good idea.

Builders don't always understand what you want when you describe your ideas and it's better if you can give them a photo, or drawing, so they have something to work from. It also saves a row if they get it wrong. Save pictures into a folder whenever you see them and use them to show decorators and builders exactly what you mean. I was forever drawing diagrams on the backs of envelopes for our builders, some get it and some don't. Sometimes, a picture really does speak a thousand words.

But it's not just about helping the builder. Creating a moodboard helps you to develop a theme, to see how the colours you like work together and whether furniture styles coordinate. You can start with an abstract picture that sums up the feeling you want to create in the room, or perhaps with a few images of rooms that you like. From there you can add paint colours – make the main colour swatch bigger than the accent ones – and then add scraps of fabric so you can see how it all fits together. It can also be worth adding a few words – perhaps describing how you want the room to feel (see Q6) – to finish off the board and keep you focused on the idea you started out with.

6

HOW DO YOU WANT THE **ROOM TO FEEL?**

This is a crucial part of interior design that often gets overlooked in favour of the colour scheme and the furniture, but thinking about how you want to feel in a room, or the feeling that you want to evoke in others, is absolutely key to helping you choose the right furniture and colours.

In the kitchen, for example, I like to feel tidy and organized so I need lots of storage and enough space on shelves so that things can be arranged without becoming too cluttered. In the living room, assuming you want a feeling of relaxation and calm, you need to work out what makes you feel that way. Personally, I am exercised if there are too many colours in one place, so I tend to stick to two with splashes of a third. I find I can't relax in a room without books, so I need those, while good lighting is key. One thing worth bearing in mind is that symmetrical arrangements are often thought to be

more calming, so when you are styling your living room, arranging matching chairs either side of the fireplace, a pair of lamps on matching tables and a candlestick on either end of the mantelpiece can be more relaxing than an eclectic mix of mismatched furniture and lots of objects. Of course, there are some for whom perfect symmetry is claustrophobic and puts them on edge.

You need to interrogate yourself about *how* you want to feel, and then work out which colours and objects will make you feel that way. This is one of those times when Pinterest can work really well. Instead of spending hours just gazing at pretty rooms and pinning colour schemes, ask yourself how your pins make you feel. Create boards based around words like 'relaxing', 'working', 'efficient' etc, then look at them and work out what the images you've pinned have got in common.

7 HOW DO I GET MY **PARTNER** TO AGREE TO MY **PLANS?**

This really is the $64,000 question, and one that I am asked all the time. There are definitely times when the role of an interior designer crosses over into couples counsellor, rather than merely showing off some wallpaper suggestions.

The Mad Husband and I mostly agree on things. We have a couple of friends – friends who are a couple – who don't agree on anything. Where he wants walls, she likes open plan; where she likes colour, he likes white. They built a house together and it was, by all accounts, a very difficult venture for all concerned. More recently they carried out a large basement conversion and rearranged the top floor of their house. I was flattered to receive an email from the husband one day asking me my opinion on various elements. This was shortly followed by a text from the wife warning me that he was planning to

talk to me and that I was to make sure that I fed back her ideas to him, as he would accept them from me, but not from her. I trod a tightrope for a few weeks there, I don't mind telling you. I also don't mind telling you that there were times when I thought they were both wrong and I gave them my own ideas regardless of tact and duplicity.

The truth is that if you have diametrically opposed tastes, there is no easy way. Marianne Shillingford, Dulux's Creative Director, swears that by the time she has cooked a steak and opened a bottle of good red wine, her husband is putty in her hands. Other women tell me they have free rein from their partners. One husband told me he just didn't care, as long as it didn't cost too much. I have always favoured the give-a-little, take-a-little approach; if you are going to ban me from the pale pink sofa of my dreams, then I will paint the spare room ceiling gold as you never go in there.

But there is often a compromise to be made. The Mad Husband loves velvet sofas. I didn't want any more velvet, but I did want the chaise longue to be reupholstered in pale pink. We met in the middle on pale pink velvet. And no it doesn't mean that we are both unhappy. For that we have the marital veto. Rarely invoked, this means that if one really can't stomach a particular idea the right to veto means it will never be mentioned again. It's final. And we've only used it about three times in 25 years so there is usually a compromise. The last time was when I wanted gold grout on the bathroom tiles. He may have been right about that. Let's go with, he wasn't completely wrong...

Sometimes it simply involves having a conversation about why an idea has been rejected. This might be fear of something being too way out, concerns of going off it, or a long-held childhood dislike of a particular colour. As I wrote in the first book, our reaction to colour is cultural, emotional and psychological – we can't always do anything about our instinctive reaction. Unearthing the reason behind a refusal is often the door to the compromise. After all, the key to successful interior design is using colours and materials to make you feel the way you want in a room, so a dislike may be based on emotional reaction rather than taste. A colour may be rejected because it recalls a hated school uniform, but that probably doesn't rule out every single shade of that colour. Or you might be able to use it in smaller doses. Referring to a moodboard (see Q5) can help someone visualize how that shade or object might look in a particular space.

Finally, if a mix of guile, seduction and reasoning is going nowhere, then there's the toddler treatment – that is, a very edited choice. What parent hasn't told their child they can have what they want for dinner as long as what they want is either red (tomato), green (pesto) or white (cheese) pasta? So put together a list of choices, all of which you can live with, but which must all be slightly different so there is a sense of a real decision being made.

It's also worth considering if one person can have a space to do entirely as they wish – it's the old 'man cave' argument. And remember, neither of you is going to be 100 per cent right every time and both of you get to have a say in what you want, so you need to be able to talk it through so that you can find the solution that you both can live with.

8

HOW DO I FIND AND CHOOSE
THE RIGHT TRADESPEOPLE?

This is the big question and we've all gone wrong on this one. My current builder, who I have known for several years, is brilliant at thinking up solutions to problems. I love that. I suggested him to a friend who didn't need that as she had an architect and a project manager and she didn't feel his attention to detail was good enough for her. So I'm very wary of recommending people now. It's tricky, because what we all want is a word of mouth recommendation, but the point is that we all have varying ideas of what constitutes affordable and what constitutes a good finish.

So find your builder, perhaps via a friend or one of those websites of recommendations, but that is only the first step. You must do your own due diligence and I appreciate that this is hard if it's your first time. Always ask for the numbers of previous clients, and call to see if you can pop round to see examples of their work – that way you can make your own judgement rather than relying on someone else's opinion. Also, it can be a good idea to ask your prospective builder if they have pictures on their phone of work they have done. This isn't a definitive

solution, but it shows a certain pride in the work carried out which counts for a lot. My builder constantly wants to show me pictures of his latest job and takes pride in doing it well.

Finally, you will have a gut instinct when you meet someone. Do you want that person turning up at 8am when you are in full chaos mode? Did you feel on meeting them that they 'got' you? Did they show initiative? What time will they start and finish? Will they work on Saturdays? I have had builders who clocked off at 3pm so they could beat the traffic and get home, but this often resulted in a half-painted floor or a part-tiled wall. I have had other builders who determined to stay late on a Friday night to finish and with whom I have shared a cold beer when the work was done.

All these things are important, and it doesn't matter if it's painting one room or redoing the whole house. It's your money and it's your instinct. What is right for one person may not be right for another, but you will only know if you ask the questions.

Whomever you choose, remember that work must meet the requirements of the building regulations.

9 WHAT CAN I DO TO MAKE A SMALL SPACE LOOK BIGGER?

Everyone wants to know the answer to this – and while there are a few tricks you can use to make your room seem bigger, just remember that what we are really talking about is the art of illusion.

Our natural instinct is to gravitate to the palest colours in small spaces, but we really don't need to. In fact, the biggest mistake we make is to assume that all skirtings, doors, picture rails, radiators and ceilings must be painted in white. A far better approach is to pick a single colour – which could be light and airy, or equally something dark and dramatic, depending on how you want your room to feel – and use it on everything. This may be a deeply challenging idea to some, but the reality is that white woodwork and ceilings will only draw attention to the edges and the exits, and the expanse (or otherwise) of the walls, and thereby heighten your awareness of the size of the room. However, painting everything the same colour blurs the edges and instantly creates a calmer feel, as well as giving the impression of pushing the walls backwards, leaving more space in the middle. Another potentially controversial idea you might consider is to paint the ceiling in gloss rather than emulsion, as that will bounce more light around from the windows.

There are various schools of thought that say playing with scale and introducing large furniture into a small space will trick people into thinking the room is bigger than it is. It *can* work but it's a hard trick to pull off, so be careful, and there are easier ways to achieve a similar effect – and I don't just advocate buying tiny cocktail chairs, by the way. Look for sofas and chairs that have narrow arms – which means more sitting space – as well as those that have taller legs so you can see the floor underneath. The more floor you see, the bigger the room feels (this also applies to wall-mounted loos and basins in bathrooms). Mid-century modern furniture fits the bill as it tends to have taller legs and wooden arms, rather than solid upholstered ones, so that light can pass through.

Try to keep your furniture slightly away from the very edges of the space, even if it's only by a couple of centimetres. Or angle a chair across a corner. That gives the impression that there was space to do that and not that everything had to hug the walls to make room for the coffee table.

While we're on the subject, think about buying a glass coffee table, or a metal one that, again, allows the light to flow through, rather than a heavy slab of wood that will dominate the space. Hang curtains all the way up to the ceiling rather than the top of the window to elongate the wall. And try to leave something empty – a corner, some wall, a space under a shelf. Empty space looks like you could afford it. It takes the pressure off and allows the room to breathe.

Mirrors are good for making a space feel bigger as they bounce light around but can also, if you have an especially large one, make the whole room feel larger by altering your perception of space and perspective. If the room is small I would tend to avoid a gallery wall, as that can bring the room in. Choose, instead, one large piece of art and make a statement. That will make the space feel bigger and calmer.

In a small kitchen, paint the cupboards the same colour as the walls to make them blend together and keep a sense of calm. Handleless cupboards will maintain a clutter-free atmosphere, and opt for flat fronts rather than Shaker-style panelling.

You should always take cupboards, and wardrobes, right up to the ceiling rather than stopping short and leaving a gap that will end up gathering dust or being filled with random stuff that only adds to the feeling of there not being enough space to store everything.

10 HOW DO I MAKE A
NARROW ROOM
LOOK WIDER?

As with Q9, this is about creating an illusion rather than actually knocking walls down, as that isn't always practical. If you live in a narrow Victorian house that has tunnel-like tendencies, then painting a doorway or the wall at the far end in a contrasting colour will bring it towards you and make the space seem squarer. Using colour this way will frame the view beyond and create a picture, rather than leaving you staring down at an endless vista. You can do the same thing by placing a focal point at the far end – a large piece of furniture in a colour that really stands out from the wall, for example. Painting the ceiling a contrasting colour to the walls and bringing the shade down, to a picture rail for example, will lower it and also help to 'square' the room.

Alternatively, try putting a sofa or a chunky chair across a long narrow room, or allowing the return arm of a modular sofa to lie across the empty space in the middle rather than fitting it into a corner. Curved sofas are becoming fashionable and can work really well in a narrow room as they take the eye towards the centre of the room rather than focusing on the edges. If your sofa is on the side of the room, matching it to the wall will allow it to blend in and recede, rather than obtruding into the narrow floor space.

It's a common mistake to arrange the furniture around the edge of a room to leave more space in the middle, as this can create the opposite effect visually. Even if the furniture is just a couple of centimetres away from the wall that will be sufficient to allow it to breathe.

If you have a narrow room, then putting two armchairs across the corners – rather than pushed up flat – allows you to see the space behind and to the sides. A chaise longue, or small sofa, lying partly across a narrow space with nothing but air behind it will do the same thing.

A square room with furniture all around the edges can look like a stage set – as if everyone is waiting for the show to start in the middle. Instead try grouping two chairs with a small table and creating a conversation corner, a low coffee table in front of a sofa and another armchair with a floor lamp in another corner.

Pulling the furniture forward also makes the (unspoken) statement that there was room to do that, that the room wasn't under such pressure that everything had to be crammed in. You are saying, with your empty space, that you could afford – metaphorically, and well perhaps financially, too – to leave that space empty.

11 HOW CAN I CREATE A
MULTI-FUNCTIONAL
ROOM?

Now that houses are getting smaller and rents are getting higher it's not uncommon to find an office in a bedroom and a bed in a living room. Even if we do have enough rooms, it's not unusual to have a living room that needs to work both as a playroom during the day and as a relaxing space at night.

So, the first thing to do is answer the six big questions at the beginning of this book so that you can properly establish just how many functions your room is going to need to fulfil. Only then can you start to consider the furniture you need to acquire. So, do you need a sofa that turns into a bed, or a desk that doubles up as a dressing table or breakfast bar? Think about buying folding chairs that you can hang on the wall when not in use – Seletti make great ones with decorated seats that are basically pop art. If you haven't got a sofa bed then buy bolsters and throws so you can dress your bed as a sofa during the day.

If you work in a room that needs to be something else, then your desk, or table, should have drawers so you can put the laptop and notebooks away.

Could the printer go in a cupboard? If you have shelves of paperwork then buy some folders that coordinate with the walls or curtains so at least they look pretty rather than just utilitarian. If you need to have a proper office chair, then why not consider having it reupholstered in some fabulous, and un-officelike material that won't affect its performance but might enhance yours.

Most of us don't have the space for large screens to divide one end of the room from another, but you might be able to use a large plant instead. Have a mix of open and closed storage so you can keep the pretty things on show and hide the practical stuff.

A table can always be used for dining and working but make sure you have thought about where the working stuff will go when the plates and glasses need to come out and vice versa. If there is room for a sideboard then you can divide the storage in half and keep one end for work and one end for pleasure. It's also worth buying a lamp that is more 'table' than 'task' so that it will look good however the room is being used.

12 HOW DO I ZONE AN OPEN-PLAN SPACE?

The architect Frank Lloyd Wright was one of the first to advocate open-plan living and his ideas were based around the idea of the kitchen as a central hub with the other spaces leading off it. The idea, says Norbert Schoenauer, in his book *6,000 Years of Housing*, was that the housewife (for that is who it was back then) could be more of a hostess in her own home rather than a 'kitchen mechanic behind closed doors'. This is an interesting and noble idea – although there was, at that time, clearly no notion of a man being a kitchen mechanic, in which case, one suspects, the walls might have come down somewhat sooner.

Be that as it may, the idea grew in popularity during the Sixties. After that, in many cities, where warehouses were converted into flats and tiny apartments were built that didn't have enough windows to allow for separate rooms, more and more people began to live in one big space rather than a series of small ones. In the UK, where many people lived in small, dark Victorian houses, it was seen as liberating to pull down the walls and open up their homes to light and shared living. Children were no longer banished to the nursery, but instead were fully functioning family members; now parents wanted to keep an eye on them – and occasionally even have a conversation with them.

This idea of open-plan living is all very well if you live alone, or in a couple. It works, up to a point, when children are small and leave you alone in the evenings when they go to bed. It all starts to go wrong when they want to hang out downstairs and listen to their own music, or watch their own TV shows. That's the point at which many despairing parents wish the walls could go back up.

Whether you happily share your space or wish you had a little more separation, there is a technique to zoning an open-plan space without having to call the builders in. It's called broken-plan living and it's the 21st-century version of the old open plan. Put simply, it has all the same benefits – the flow of light, the open spaces, the shared living – but it's about zoning one large space into small areas for different activities and moods. It's like living in separate rooms that don't have walls.

First, decide on the different areas that you need to accommodate. Usually that will be a kitchen, a dining area and a living and relaxing area. The easiest way to achieve the broken-plan effect is with rugs. Work out how much space you need for your sofa and chairs

and buy a rug that sits fully under all of the furniture in that area. By changing the floor you will immediately demarcate that zone. The rug does the job of the walls. By introducing a new texture – wool instead of wood, for example – you are signalling that that area is different from the ones around it. In this case softer, cosier, and intended for relaxation.

If the space is large, think about putting a self-contained tiled floor in the kitchen area, and running natural wood throughout the rest of the living and dining area. If it's small or long and thin, then keep it uniform. If you rent, or can't change the floors, then vary the texture of the rugs – wool in the sitting area and raffia, or even recycled plastic, in the dining space. Can you put a round one under the table, and a rectangular one by the sofa? Changing the shapes will also change the zone.

So now you have three different floor areas. The next way to divide the space is open shelving. If the space is large enough you can sit a shelving unit with no back on it between two areas. Then put some books facing one way and some the other, add a few ornaments and objets and you have created a low-level dividing wall through which light is able to flow easily around the room. You can do the same thing with plants. If you can grow tall ones, then make a wall of them. If you don't have green fingers (or thumbs) use fake ones. If you have small plants, try putting them on a narrow console table to add height.

If you are planning a refurbishment or a new kitchen and have space, an island will do the same job as a low-level wall. Add some bar stools and make sure they have their backs to the rest of the room. That is another way to zone a big space – turn your back on parts of it. Likewise when you have placed your large rug under the sofa, make sure the sofa has its back to the kitchen, or dining area, or is facing the garden. In an open-plan space you should put furniture in the middle rather than around the edge – that will help create a notion of separateness.

Finally, make sure you have different lighting in each area. Don't feel that a pendant light has to be in the middle of the room. Instead hang it over the dining table. Put downlights over the kitchen and table and floor lamps in the seating area. This will enable you to zone the space further by varying both functionality and atmosphere.

Now you may live in a single large space, but you have created a sense of separate rooms. And the same way of thinking will achieve a similar effect in a teenager's bedroom or a studio flat, where you may want to create a desk area and a sitting space that is separate from the sleeping zone, for example. These tricks will work on any scale and in any open-plan or multi-functional living space.

13 HOW **BIG** SHOULD
THE **RUG BE?**

As big as you can afford. A small rug floating in the middle of a room creates an island that no man wants to walk on. The front legs of your sofa should always be on a rug. In an open-plan space use a rug to zone a whole area by making sure that all the relevant pieces of furniture are sitting on it (see Q12).

If you can't afford a giant rug, buy a large piece of carpet – patterned is good as it will look more like a rug – and have the edges hemmed, perhaps in a contrasting colour. Position it on a piece of underlay (a good idea with any rug to stop it 'walking') and you're done. We used this trick with a carpet remnant that cost about £100 to buy and the same again to hem. A rug in the equivalent size would have cost upwards of £1,000.

Layering rugs is tricky. It's about mixing patterns (see Q29), but in essence you need the colours to work together tonally. It's easy enough to mix lots of Persian rugs – think Gaddafi's tent – but one easy trick that is an affordable way of covering space is to use the famous black-and-white-striped Stockholm rug from Ikea as your base; it will work in conjunction with just about any other rug you choose. You simply overlap one side of it (don't stick it in the middle) with a plain mustard colour, for example. Or how about a bold floral number, and then a plain rug in one of the colours from the floral design. Just make sure that you aren't layering lots of particularly thick-pile rugs, or your furniture will start to wobble. Use carpet glue and furniture to stop your rug arrangement slipping and sliding.

14 WHEN CAN I PUT A **RUG** **ON TOP** OF THE CARPET?

Never. It doesn't really work and not just for stylistic reasons. Firstly, the whole arrangement becomes quite high, so you need to keep it away from doors as they won't open and you don't want coffee tables and chairs to wobble. Also, rugs tend to 'walk' more when they're laid on top of carpet.

But that's just the practical side. It's just not a great look either. If you're in rented accommodation and you're trying to cover up a hideous carpet then I totally get it. You gotta do what you gotta do. In which case buy the biggest rug you can afford and cover up as much of the carpet as you can – remember to check if the door will open over the top or if you need to allow clearance.

If a large rug is beyond the budget, then consider buying a large piece of carpet and hemming it (see Q13), then you can simply lay it over the top and take it with you when you leave. If you love rugs but your floorboards are beyond salvation, then lay sisal or seagrass and arrange rugs over the top. It's a change of texture, so it can work – but again, don't forget to check your door openings.

15 WHAT **SHAPE** RUG SHOULD I BUY?

For the most part rugs are rectangular, and that seems to work quite well. A square one is fine in a large square room but beware of putting a small square in a large rectangle. Round rugs are best left to jute, sisal and natural materials that can look great on a flagstone floor, although they're terrible crumb huggers.

An odd-shaped rug like a sheepskin, can work well by the side of the bed as they are also soft to step on when you get up. For the exception to the rug island rule (see Q13), I think you can have a cowhide rug – or even a zebra skin – under your coffee table. The irregular shape takes away from the 'island-iness' of it.

16

WHERE CAN I FIND MORE
STORAGE SPACE?

No one has enough storage. Victoria Beckham doesn't have enough storage. The Queen probably doesn't have enough storage. The simple truth is that the stuff you own will expand to fit the space available. And when it's filled the space available, it will spill out onto the chairs and over the end of the sofa and into little piles dotted around the house. So the first thing you need to do, before you start complaining that you don't have enough storage, is to have a bit of a declutter. Often it's not that the house is too small, but the piles of stuff are too big. That done, it's time to start looking at where you can put the things you *do* actually need.

First rule of thumb: when the floor is full, use the walls. This works very well in a bathroom – shelves and slimline cupboards are perfect in here. They only need to be one bottle deep, too.

Walls full? What about under the stairs? That's a handy little spot that isn't doing much.

Many people build bookshelves around doorways. This is good if you have a lot of paperbacks as the shelves can be narrow, and you won't feel like you are walking through a tunnel.

In the kitchen, and the bedroom come to that, make sure that any storage you build in goes all the way up to the ceiling. Not only will this make

the room look taller but when you stop the cupboards a foot below the ceiling you're just making a space to store dust. At least box it in fully so you can keep all the stuff you never use dust free. Under the bed is another good place to store things, but it's terrible for the feng shui – blocks the chi – and you wouldn't believe how much dust comes out of a mattress. But if needs must then invest in those vacuum storage bags which will (a) shrink anything soft so you can store more, and (b) keep the dust, and by extension the moths, off.

Period houses often have lots of odd little spaces to store things in. Alcoves, triangles formed by sloping ceilings, funny sticky-outy bits. Walk around your place now and see if you can identify any that could be filled with shelves and storage. And if your rooms are all plain squares then that's also great – see if you can create a wall of storage with a row of flat-fronted handleless doors, painted to match the wall, that almost disappears. Imagine if it was as narrow as the ironing board. Could you afford to lose that much space in a room? Because you would gain a huge amount of cupboard space. And, if it was mostly filled with things you didn't need that much (yes, the ironing board in my case), you could

Based on @thefrugality

certainly put furniture in front of it (an armchair if not a sofa) and be able to move it to get at the contents.

Landings are also good spaces for storage. There usually isn't enough room for actual furniture, yet it needs only to be big enough to allow two people to go up and down. Add some narrow shelves for books here and free up space elsewhere. A word of warning on that, though… The owners of our previous home had done exactly that on a wall of the stairs at the very top of the house. They had also added a skylight. When we moved out six years later, the spines of all our books had faded completely and now the only way to know which book is which is to start reading it, which isn't conducive to getting anything else done…

17
WHAT DO I NEED TO KNOW
ABOUT CARPET?

I know that carpet suffers from a slight image problem for many of you, but the fact remains that most of us have some of it, and it still accounts for 57 per cent of all the flooring sold in the UK. Some of the remaining 43 per cent is laminate and that is a banned word on these pages unless it's preceded by the words, 'how to replace'.

But carpet in the bedroom is soft and warm and, crucially, noise-reducing for anyone in the room below. Wool carpet is also naturally flame resistant which is another reason to consider it. It is harder to set fire to (from a fallen candle or dropped cigarette) and gives off fewer harmful fumes than synthetic materials. Finally, it absorbs heat and releases it slowly, meaning it will help warm your home in winter and regulate temperatures in summer.

A very common misapprehension is that asthmatics and allergy sufferers are better off with floorboards than carpet. The truth is that floorboards – particularly old ones with gaps between the boards – mean dust is constantly floating around, whereas carpet traps and holds dust particles, preventing them from aggravating delicate air passages. Obviously, you will still need to vacuum regularly to remove that dust, but at least it's out of the way in the meantime.

Those are the pros. Of course, there are cons – it's just not that fashionable – but sometimes there is no choice. Not all of us have the luxury of wooden floorboards downstairs – and it's much cheaper to lay carpet than parquet. So if you are forced into carpet or have chosen it for upstairs, read on.

18 WHAT **CARPET** FOR WHICH **ROOM?**

Stair carpet needs to be hardwearing so a twist or a cut pile is a good choice as it's more resistant to crushing than, say, a loop carpet. A mix of 80 per cent wool and 20 per cent nylon is also a good choice for stairs. The reason for this is that the nylon toughens up the wool and this mix is three to four times tougher than wool on its own, which is why it's good for high traffic areas.

You can have wool – which takes rich colour really well – in the bedroom where there isn't so much footfall. But wool carpet will mark from the legs of furniture unless you buy furniture coasters. These come in a variety of materials – mine are plastic but look like Bakelite, and once they're on you really don't notice them.

If you have dogs or cats who scratch, make sure you don't buy a loop carpet. As the name suggests if you pull one strand of a loop the whole lot unravels. That is why a cut carpet, where all the threads are individual, is better.

If you choose a pattern, you might need to buy more to match this across joins, or in rooms that are unusually shaped. On stairs with half landings or winders (curving around floors) you will need more to cope with the change in direction and how the pile lies.

Oh, and don't forget the cost of the underlay and fitting, although sometimes they will throw the underlay in for free. Always ask.

19 HOW DO I
CLEAN A CARPET?

The key is to act fast. Use a blotting or a dabbing action rather than scrubbing and rubbing. If you do that the pile will burst and you may remove the spillage but end up with a fluffy patch that is lighter in appearance, so there will still be a mark, even if it isn't red wine.

If you've really made a mess then it's probably best to consult a professional. There's even an app for this now (of course there is) – Woolsafe Carpet Cleaning Apps.

You may have read about, or even tried, such tricks as spraying club soda onto a stain; or throwing salt on top of red wine – which I have tried and just ended up with a purple stain rather than a red one; or that other old favourite, pouring white wine on to red to neutralize it. Don't do it. Instead, soak with absorbent tissue and dab (I said dab, don't rub!) with a white cloth moistened with some carpet shampoo. (I know, you haven't got any. Go and buy some now. You'll be glad you did.) Blot again, and/or use a wet suction vacuum if you have one, then dab with warm water on a clean cloth and blot, or suck up, the remaining moisture. When dry, brush the pile back.

If you have dents in the carpet from your furniture, and you didn't buy the coasters from Q18, then some people have reported success with ice cubes. You leave the cold water to melt slightly into the fibres, and this can help restore the original shape. Others suggest that laying a damp kitchen towel over the dent and running a steam iron gently over the top will help. It's not always possible but if you can move the furniture two or three centimetres to the side and back again every now and then that will help.

20 WHAT IS THE DIFFERENCE BETWEEN LINO AND VINYL?

Many of you probably think these are two words for the same product and, I'll admit, so did I until I started looking into them. Well, I had a vague notion that one belonged to the 1970s and one had become fashionable in recent years. Beyond that I had no idea. However, it turns out that vinyl is man-made using petroleum, which is non-renewable, while linoleum is made from linseed, which is extracted from flaxseeds and which is then mixed with other natural substances such as cork dust and wood flour.

In terms of the pros and cons...

Vinyl can be waterproof and is good for damp areas whereas lino is water resistant and needs sealing from time to time. Excessive humidity can also cause lino edges to curl.

Vinyl patterns are now created by photographic images being printed onto the surface, which can look extremely realistic. Lino tends to have designs embedded all the way through, which limits the patterns available, but means it won't fade.

Both are relatively easy to install and both will last a minimum of 10 years although linoleum can last up to 40.

21 WHAT IS ENGINEERED WOOD?

Engineered wood is made from lots of layers of wood and you can choose the top layer in the look you want – oak or walnut for example. It tends to be fitted by being clicked together or slotted in a tongue and groove system.

It is not to be confused with laminate as it has real wood on the top layer rather than a picture of real wood. Engineered wood also works really well with underfloor heating. It is much more complicated to install underfloor heating if you have original floorboards (individual pieces of wood laid over a series of joists with a gap underneath, also known as a suspended floor), as the cables need to be fixed individually to the side of each joist. A point to note: if you are fitting underfloor heating (see Q23) be aware that you can inadvertently delaminate your engineered wood if you have it turned up too high with a thick rug on top.

Solid wood flooring is a modern version of floorboards in that you can have it fitted without gaps underneath so you won't get draughts and dust. It looks amazing and you can buy wide boards and a wide range of finishes. It's expensive though.

22 WHAT ABOUT PARQUET?

Parquet is flooring made from small blocks of wood laid in a geometric pattern. It's highly decorative and, like floorboards, can be sourced on eBay in its original form, but be prepared to have to clean each block and to get specialist help in laying it. Parquet has come strongly back into fashion in recent years but be mindful that it's expensive both to buy and to install. This explains why some people are now opting for vinyl versions (see Q20), which are created by photographing the real thing, meaning that it can be hard to tell if it's real wood or not by sight. Touching and walking on it (it's more cushioned than wood) will give the game away, of course.

23 WHAT DO I NEED TO KNOW ABOUT **UNDERFLOOR HEATING?**

Underfloor heating is certainly gaining popularity, and not just because it is thought to be more efficient at heating the room, but because it also frees up valuable wall space, which makes furnishing the room easier.

There are no cold spots with underfloor heating, unlike a radiator, which will heat the immediate area (meaning you often have a hot spot directly in front of it and a cold spot in the middle of the room). In addition, you would tend to leave underfloor heating on at a steady temperature all the time – say 20°C (68°F) during the day and 18°C (64°F) at night or when you are out. This contrasts with the limited hours – morning and night – you would use radiator systems, which are both more wasteful and more expensive as they demand a massive surge of energy to get up to temperature.

There are basically two types of underfloor heating – water and electric. To find out more, I consulted Tom Pike, a developer and project manager who also spent 20 years 'on the tools', so he knows what he's talking about.

Water-based systems break down into three types. The first, where you lay pipes into concrete, cover with a smooth screed and lay the flooring over the top is best for new builds or extensions where you are starting from the beginning. However, it activates relatively slowly as you have to heat the screed before the heat reaches the flooring and pushes out from there.

The second type can be retrofitted under floorboards, which might be the best solution for a period property where the floor is suspended over joists. This involves taking up all the boards, insulating the spaces underneath and then fitting the heating pipes to the sides of the joists. The insulation is key so that you're not heating the ground but the room above. There's a lot of work involved, so it's expensive in terms of labour.

The final option is an overlay, which is the cheapest to install, but there are side effects. The heating system is simply laid over the existing floor, and a new floor is laid over the top. This will raise the floor by at least 40mm (1½in) and means you may have to plane all the doors to open over the new levels. And there are other undesirable consequences, too. For example, if you are doing the whole of the downstairs, the bottom step on the staircase may suddenly feel too low and if you have already installed your kitchen, the work surface will also feel lower. If you are installing this type of flooring before you change the kitchen, or if you need to install a new staircase anyway, then you can factor this in. But do walk around and look at the different flooring levels in your house beforehand, because if you only want to do one room you will be creating a step down into the next one.

If you are only planning on doing a small area, such as a bathroom, shower area or kitchen, then electric might be a better option. It's easier (therefore cheaper) to install and works well under both wooden and tiled floors.

You should ask your builder (and a manufacturer) what type they would recommend for your property. It's worth noting that while electricity is currently more expensive than gas (which is probably what will power a water-based system), the growth of wind and solar energy may ultimately bring the price down and could make this a carbon neutral option, which the water system is unlikely ever to be.

Finally, if you have decided on underfloor heating, then don't buy heavy, deep-pile rugs or the heat won't penetrate.

One more tip: if you are installing an electric system in the bathroom, do consider fitting an extra panel behind the wall and adding a couple of hooks. It will heat the room more efficiently than a towel rail, as well as drying your towels.

HOW TO PLAN A KID'S ROOM: A CHECKLIST

You cannot expect a room to take a child through from nursery to 18. Roughly speaking, there is the newborn nursery phase, which will last until they go to school. This can be tweaked towards the end of primary or, at a pinch, when they start secondary school. In my experience they will want a change at around five and again at 12. This can then be altered a little at around 14, which, if you do it right, will take them right through the teenage years.

☐ On the basis that you will need to make changes roughly every five years, plan your budget accordingly. Clearly the newborn phase, which is the shortest, should be the cheapest – but there's no accounting for the amount of money excited new parents can spend on stuff they don't really need.

☐ Do you really have to have a fancy changing table? Surely a regular table, with storage drawers, will do. Consider a low chest of drawers with a changing mat on top. My sons were changed on what was basically my desk while I was on maternity leave.

☐ A word on colour. Yellow is very stimulating – think carefully before you bathe a nursery in this sunny colour if you are hoping for good sleep patterns. Grey is not a joyful colour, however neutral it seems.

☐ If the budget is tight, resist the desire to buy tiny desks and chairs – they will grow out of them so fast. Also, they will mostly play on the floor until they are about 10 so don't buy a desk at all until then.

☐ The smaller the child, the bigger the toys. By the end of primary school the huge playhouses, trucks and boxes of building bricks will be mostly redundant and replaced by tiny screens that don't take up much room.

☐ Carpet is good as they spend so much time on the floor, but if you hate carpet then buy a really big rug to put over seagrass or floorboards. Either way, it will get stained and ruined. Don't spend a fortune.

☐ Once they go to secondary school, they will spend more time in their bedrooms with their mates. A desk, a couple of beanbags and a daybed that can double as a sofa are all good ideas at this stage.

continued >>>

Layout & Flooring

☐ The best storage solution I have found is to line the walls with Shaker pegs. They can hang clothes (either individually or on hangers), bags of toys, bags of hair accessories, pictures on string, hats, spare chairs etc. And it's much easier to fling something on a hook than fold it into a drawer. Trust me on this – I have the messiest teenager you will ever, ever meet.

☐ Give them ownership. If you are frightened of what colour they will choose, then edit a selection that you like first and present them with that (see Q7).

PAINTING & DECORATING

24 WHAT DO I DO ABOUT ROUGH WALLS AND HOLES?

One of the reasons that professional decorators are expensive is because they will do the preparation really well. If you have MDF shelves installed, for example, a professional will sand them, fill where the screw holes are, sand again, seal them and only then start painting. If it's me, I've slapped the paint on as the carpenter is closing the door behind him.

When it comes to walls, preparation is key. You should fill all the tiny cracks and holes and sand them before painting. Keenos will also talk about sugar-soaping walls to clean them. If your walls have any stains from historic damp (I'm going to assume that if you have actual damp you are going to deal with it first) you need to cover them with Zinsser B-I-N, which is a primer that seals and blocks all stains and stops them coming back through after you have finished painting. Apply that first and then paint as normal.

And this seems like a good moment to mention the equipment. An angled brush is good for corners and, well, angles. Use a brush to outline the edges (cutting in) and fill in the bigger spaces with a roller. Some people don't like rollers – and it's true that they can leave a sort of dimpled effect – but they are much faster and work the paint in well. Rollers do splash, so cover everything before you start.

25 WHAT PAINT DO I USE FOR WHICH SURFACE?

When I suggested this book to my publisher, I was thinking about this question. I wanted to compile the most commonly asked questions from the blog and this is, by far and away, the thing I am asked the most. What paint goes on the skirting boards? Can I use the same paint on the walls as the woodwork? What is gloss for? And eggshell? And so on. So here goes…

Let's start with walls – the largest area. Emulsion is the name of the game here. That's the standard wall paint. The key thing you need to look out for is the percentage of sheen. In recent years, the trend has been for ultra-flat matt paint with a slightly chalky finish. This is because it holds the colour really well and gives a wonderfully soft, almost powdery, finish. This is the paint that will change with the light which means that sometimes it can look almost velvety. This is the paint that makes it so hard to find the exact shade you want because it changes according to the weather, the climate and the time of day. It's beautiful stuff.

But it's not tough. You put this in your hall at your own peril because it attracts fingerprints and black marks and can chip easily too. And you can't wipe it down. Shall I say that again? You can't wipe it down. So it's not the most practical in high traffic areas – by

which I mean halls and stairs etc.

These chalky paints will typically only have two or three per cent sheen. But, in their favour is that they will have the effect of smoothing down the wall and hiding any lumps and bumps. So you may have to trade between smooth-looking walls and fingerprints.

If you want something more practical – for the kitchen or bathroom for example – look for paints with a higher sheen, or words like 'modern emulsion', 'humidity paint', 'marble' and 'intelligent'. This isn't an exhaustive list but it's a start. One example: Dulux has an Easycare range that protects against mould and is grease and stain-resistant – the marks form into beads that can be wiped off. It's based on the hydrophobic qualities of leaves. It's always worth picking something with a sheen for the hall, stairs and landings, too, as they are constantly getting scuffed from passing traffic.

Gloss used to be the thing for woodwork but it has slightly fallen out of fashion. Its toughness is part of the reason it was so popular, and it stretches slightly, which is good for wood as it expands and contracts with changes in temperature. But these days eggshell, which is more matt and less tough, is fashionable. You pays yer money and you takes yer chances.

Gloss requires longer to dry: it all used to be oil-based but that's no longer the case. Now you can get water-based paints in all finishes. But beware of white oil-based gloss, which contains resins that yellow over time. A water-based white gloss will stay white for longer.

Remember I said you wanted emulsion for walls? Well that's all changed now. These days you don't have to use gloss just on woodwork. Its shine and durability means that it will bounce light around, so if you choose a dark colour it can work really well in a gloss finish. Gloss is also good on ceilings. It's harder to use but when well applied it can look like an expensive lacquer. As gloss is so easy to keep clean it can also look really good on the lower half of a wall – in the hall for example. You could paint the lower half in gloss and the top half in the same colour, but matt (see Q39). Doing this with the traditional dividing line of a dado rail looks really modern and is also a great way to add character to a new build where you might not have any interesting features to play with. I have painted the small bathroom in my loft entirely in navy blue gloss (apart from the tiled bit). It looks wonderful, the water and condensation doesn't upset it and it reflects the light back from the roof light brilliantly.

When it comes to painting radiators, you can probably find metal paint or, if you want to match them to the wall – and you do – then two or three coats of eggshell will do the job perfectly.

You can also buy special paint for tiles, which can be brilliant for renters (landlords permitting) or anyone who doesn't have the budget for a full retiling job. The key is in the preparation and doing it carefully. It may also be a good idea to scrape out any dirty, old grout and replace it, or try using a whitening pen to freshen it up. If you don't like the colour of tile paint you can use a primer followed by a gloss paint for a tough finish.

Lastly, floors. You need floor paint. I have used water-based floor paint from Farrow & Ball and it's not as tough as an oil-based paint from, say, Little Greene, but it dries faster, which is a major consideration when you are already living in a house. If I were starting again, or had yet to move in, I think I might choose an oil-based paint for the floors. Some people recommend Ronseal DiamondHard Floor Paint, which is acrylic but is only available in a limited palette of 10 basic colours – including white, cream, black, slate, olive green and terracotta – and many of us are looking for a little more subtlety of shade than that.

26 HOW DO I PAINT uPVC DOORS AND WINDOWS?

It used to be that once you had plastic windows you were stuck with them. In their favour is the fact that they are pretty good at keeping draughts out. While you can get used to the look of a window and, to some extent, hide it on the inside with curtains etc, a big old slab of plastic front door isn't anyone's idea of pretty.

But you *can* paint them. Start with something like Ronseal One Coat All Surface Primer and Undercoat. You can either paint it on or buy a spray and, as the advert famously asserts, it actually does what it says on the tin. It is also recommended that you sand the uPVC lightly first (use 1200 grade paper) to create a 'key' for the primer to stick to. Wipe it down with a damp cloth and away you go. You then use normal paint over the top once it's fully dry. This primer will also work on metal, by the way (but not rust).

PlastiKote spray takes longer to dry. If you are doing windows, you will need to tape up the glass really well or remove the panes if possible. The trouble with a long drying time is that if you are painting the front door you will need it to be dry before you can close it that night, so the first option may be better.

Your final option is Zinsser AllCoat Exterior paint, which claims to need no priming and no sanding and to be ready for a second coat in one hour. In fact, it dries so fast that some people find that a disadvantage as it doesn't give you long to work. Make sure you paint in neat strokes in the same direction and sand over any lumpy areas. Then try a thin third coat. You probably won't get rid of the brush strokes but some people say that makes the surface look more grainy and wood-like.

27 HOW TO USE
SPRAY PAINT

Sometimes you see the perfect light, and it's silver when you wanted gold, or you've spent a fortune on brass taps and can't find a matching shower drain. Spraying can work really well – even on components that are to be exposed to water – but it can be tricky to get right. Tania James, also known as Ms Quirk, one half of design team Quirk and Rescue, often uses spray paint and shares her advice here:

TANIA JAMES
A.K.A MS QUIRK

Firstly make sure you work outside – airborne paint particles are extremely difficult to remove from other pieces of furniture and walls.

Wear a mask as the fumes will be strong – another very good reason to make sure you work outside.

The item must be cleaned and primed – I use a spray that makes everything white to begin with, which is a good base.

It's easier if you stand your object on a plinth – you could try an upturned paint pot covered in a plastic bag – that way you can spray all visible surfaces quite easily.

It's always better to do two or three thin coats. The first one should be thin enough that you can still see the primer. Holding it too close, or spraying too thickly will result in drips. Try to stay about 15cm (6in) away and use a damp cloth straight away to wipe the drips off. If you don't spot them until it's dry, you can sand them off with fine grade sandpaper.

Leave each coat to dry fully before starting the next. This may involve leaving it overnight.

I like Rust-Oleum, which comes in lots of different finishes including high gloss, matt and satin. But if the object you want to spray already has a very shiny finish – glossy plastic for example – then try a hardcore primer (available from Halfords) meant for cars. This might only come in grey, so when it's dry you will still need the regular primer in white to cover the grey and make a good base.

28 HOW DO YOU CREATE A COHESIVE COLOUR SCHEME?

I am asked this all the time and while I think for the most part it will find itself, there are a few techniques to making sure the whole house hangs together. You will tend to be drawn to a colour palette that works within itself and to an overriding decorative style that works together. I have bits of pink in every room, for example – from the walls of the bedroom to the cushions in the living room, and the burgundy spotty stair carpet.

And there you have the key element. The stairs – if you have them – are the backbone of the house. Everything flows from there, so that can be the central colour. If you live in a flat and don't have stairs, then it can be the hall or wherever you enter from. If that is your favourite colour, then you can ensure that you include elements of it in every other room.

So, you might have – as I do – a white hall with a burgundy spotty stair carpet. That leads to the living room – painted chocolate brown but with burgundy Persian rugs on white floorboards. The kitchen has chocolate brown cupboards with a single pink wall and sliding pantry door. There are also some pink plates. Upstairs the bedroom is painted pale pink with a dark green wall behind the bed and matching shelves, and in the en suite bathroom, it's dark green with a pale pink fireplace and window frame.

Sophie Robinson, my podcasting co-host, adores cobalt blue. Her hall is painted in that colour, which is strong and dramatic. She has a white office leading off it and a pale pink living room with a cobalt blue sofa, so the elements of blue flow throughout the house – and her wardrobe I might add.

It's about picking one colour – and it doesn't have to be a neutral – and working it in throughout your home. So either coat some walls in it and use it sparingly elsewhere or make sure, if you prefer neutral walls, that the sofa, the bedspread, a picture in the kitchen and the dining chairs are all linked with a splash of that colour. It doesn't have to be the same throughout, just a variant, so that it's not too matching.

My house ranges from deepest burgundy to the palest of blush pinks, but they all go together tonally. The colours in other rooms include green, grey, chocolate, ecru, chalky white and navy blue. Oh, and there's a metallic gold ceiling in my office.

29 HOW TO MIX COLOURS AND PATTERNS

A design scheme will be more individual if it isn't *too* matching (which can look as if you just went to one website and added everything to cart), so it's worth knowing how to get this right.

First up, you need to make sure the colours work tonally. Consult a paint chart if you're not sure about this. For example, the colours on a Farrow & Ball chart all go together as they are from the same palette. If you added a clean bright shade from Dulux it would throw the whole thing off.

One new design idea gathering pace is to mix paint colours within a room – this is known as colour blocking. For example, Bianca Hall from French for Pineapple has painted a contrasting colour square to frame a series of prints hanging in her dining room. Another trick is to paint a wide stripe behind the bed going up over the ceiling to create the effect of a canopy. If you have a palette of toning colours you can even paint different coloured shapes on the walls and ceiling – Mary le Comte of MoseyHome has painted a series of contrasting squares and triangles to make the ceiling of her son's bedroom a point of interest.

Once you are tonally on the same page, you can mix different patterns together and it will work. So you might look for bold florals, a couple of plains in different colours, and one with a more graphic image. You can always include stripes and geometric patterns. Muted florals can look great next to a black and white stripe, while a black and white geometric will work well next to some neon tones. Have a play around until you have found a combination that works.

When it comes to cushions, you want to mix the shapes and sizes around, too. If it's rugs, then it's a little trickier – although you can mix Persian rugs with impunity as the colours and motifs tend to blend (see Q13). But I wouldn't mix a modern geometric with a Persian rug. That's tricky.

30 WHAT ABOUT **WHITE?**

The thing about white is that it's a default colour. Not sure what to pick? Paint it white. Now I don't have an issue with it, and there is a lot of white (and by white I mean chalky not brilliant) in my own house. What I take issue with is the mechanical nature of the decision. Is your ceiling white because you wanted it to be, or because the builder assumed you wanted white? Same goes for the woodwork.

As I've written before, if you're stuck on a colour scheme, then look to your wardrobe. And here's my question: do you always wear a white shirt, no matter what is on the bottom half? I'm guessing not. You might have pink or green or yellow, or stripes. You pick a colour to go with a pair of trousers according to the shade you think will go best. So a cobalt blue room might look amazing if the ceiling was a very, very pale shade of pink. That pink might also go with a deep dark red or a foresty green. In my office the walls, door and woodwork are all pale pink, the fireplace is burgundy and the ceiling is gold. There is no white at all.

If you have a very small room that you don't feel confident painting dark, then how about choosing a pale colour, but paint the whole room – woodwork, walls and ceiling. That is the route we took, and we even extended it to the floors as well. It makes a small room look bigger, as you aren't drawing attention to the edges and the confines of the space.

Instead of pale pink you might prefer to choose a delicate blue or a stone colour that is warmer. And if you do like to contrast the woodwork then you can do that, too. It doesn't have to match the walls, but if it's going to contrast then pick two colours that like each other rather than just defaulting to traditional white.

Look at things in your wardrobe that are patterned and examine the colour combinations. Pink walls with a pale ochre ceiling will look amazing. Or make that burgundy and gold (I am thinking of my summer trousers as I write here), but you could also have navy walls with a mint green ceiling. You get the idea. I'm not banning white – but I am saying don't go white until you've thought about it first.

31 HOW DO I **PICK** THE RIGHT **COLOUR?**

I can't give the definitive answer for you personally, but I can tell you where to look for it. I always instruct clients to look at their wardrobe first. The colours you like to wear will be the colours you are comfortable living in. This doesn't work for everyone, all the time, but it's usually a pretty good guide. However, if what you find there is a bright colour that you don't want to plaster all over the walls, perhaps you could paint the ceiling, or buy a chair or a cushion in that shade, and extend the colour scheme from there.

Picking paint colours *is* hard, so it helps to have a starting point from a cushion or a piece of furniture that you know will ultimately be used in the room. Another starting point can be a favourite painting, or perhaps a place you have visited that made you feel happy. Think back to the colours you saw there and which ones you liked best. If you're not sure what colours will work with your starter colour then go either to a fabric shop and browse through the pattern books to get ideas for colour combinations, or look at wallpaper designs online. You never know, you might even end up with a paper or fabric that you want to use.

You will need to test your colour in situ, as the final shade will vary depending on the light – cool blue north, warm golden south – and if you are seeing it under natural or electric light. Try it first – and remember it's only paint and it's easy to change if you get it wrong. And we all have.

Last year I persuaded The Mad Husband that we should paint our spare room ceiling gold. Actually he was relatively up for that. We then decided to do the top half of our walls in pale blush, and a deep burgundy below the dado rail – to loosely tie with our burgundy stair carpet. I then had to go away for three days for work while the room was being decorated. I texted from the airport on my way home to ask how it looked: 'Bit 1970s Indian Restaurant', came the reply. And I didn't need to see it to know that he was right. We spent the weekend painting over the burgundy with more of the pale pink and I loved it so much that I decided it was no longer the spare room – it was my office. By the Sunday evening I had bought a desk from eBay and the following week I had moved in.

So don't worry if you make a mistake. It happens to us all, and yes it's time spent redoing it, or paying the decorator, but it will be worth it in the end. There's nothing worse than a room that you don't want to use because it's the wrong colour.

32

WHEN IS
EXPENSIVE PAINT
WORTH THE MONEY?

The short answer is nearly always. Unless you decorate all the time, in which case it's just not worth spending hundreds of pounds on paint because it's only on the wall for a year before it changes again. For everyone else? Yes, it's worth it.

Firstly, the pigments in expensive paint come from natural sources, like rocks and minerals, which have complex structures. That's why they appear to change in the light according to the time of day and the weather outside. It's infuriating when you're trying to find the right shade of grey, but fabulous when you've nailed it. Walls coated in richly pigmented paints made up of many colours can seem almost velvety in the sunlight.

Cheaper paints, while consistent in colour, just don't have that quality. They are flatter. They will have less pigment, which may well be synthetic, and more water. For that reason, it's often a bad idea to go for a colour-matching service. The matching can be hit and miss – I tried it once to recreate an archived shade of green and the result – which still cost me £30 – was unusable. This also means that should you need to mix more (if you run out or need to touch up) you may not get the right colour.

So yes, good paint costs more money. If you find the colour you like in a cheaper range then definitely use it for high traffic areas like halls, stairs and landings. They need regular painting and cleaning, whatever the quality of the paint. And while we're on the subject of cleaning – the flat chalky paint beloved by so many of us will mark. It's hard to clean and it's not practical in a high-traffic area. Choose a modern emulsion instead, which will have a slight sheen that you can wipe clean. Or marry a painter. (See Q25 for what paint to use on which surface.)

However, when it comes to living rooms and bedrooms, it's worth splashing out on expensive paint, as you will enjoy a depth of colour that you won't achieve with cheaper names.

Now, you may hear expensive brands telling you that you will use less of their product so it's worth it against cheaper paints. I'm not sure I buy that. In these days of water-based, low-VOC (volatile organic compounds) paints, it seems they all need a few coats to stick – and the more coats you apply, the deeper and richer the colour will be.

Talking of chemicals, it's worth mentioning that eco-paints are gaining popularity as we become more aware of disposing of the leftovers and the empty tins, the chemicals within, and what they may be doing to us and to the planet.

In the same way that organic food is increasingly a choice that only the affluent can afford to make, perhaps expensive paint is that, too. So if your budget won't stretch to the expensive brands, at least get the colour right so you don't have to keep redoing it.

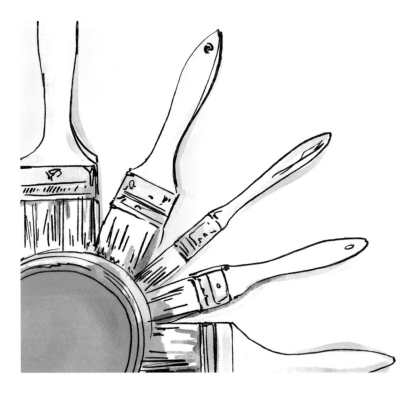

33 WHY SHOULD I BUY
TESTER POTS?

You cannot tell what a paint colour is like from a computer screen as all computers are calibrated differently. What looks grey on mine might be blue on yours. A soft chalky white on mine, dirty green on yours. So, that is the first reason.

The second is that you have no idea how the colour will look in your room until you have tried it. It will change enormously depending on whether you are seeing it in the cool blue northern light or the warm yellow glow from the south. It will change enormously depending on the colour of the sofa in front of it or the floor it meets at the bottom. I spent ages trying to find the right blush pink for my bedroom and hating them all as they were too peachy. It wasn't until, two years later, having defaulted to grey, that I tested one with a violet undertone and found it was perfect in a south-facing room. We also used some in the north-facing en suite, where it was quite different – much cooler in tone.

Some years ago, I visited a client's house. She wanted some finishing touches for her bedroom and spare room. We walked into her large south-facing room with its brass light fittings and huge French bed. The colour on the walls was breathtaking – a sort of pale delicate shadow of a blue. It was Borrowed Light by Farrow & Ball, described by the manufacturer as the colour of summer sky when it cascades through a small window. It was truly stunning. We floated about talking duvet covers and bedside tables and then moved into the room behind – the spare room.

'Gosh,' I said, 'I see what you mean about this room. It feels really cold and unwelcoming doesn't it. What colour is this?' There was a pause. You guessed it. Borrowed Light was the reply... Tester pots. That's why you need to buy them.

And these are just the changes you get from natural light coming in different directions. You also need to see what happens to the paint colour between daylight and the electric light of the evening.

And, in case you're not convinced, it's not just the light that changes things. Paint will often react to the furniture around it. Particularly grey. If you have ended up with a cold grey, then adding lots of natural wood to the room will do wonders to warm it up. A grey that has gone beige in a south or west light can be cooled down with black and silver.

Tester pots. You need to buy them.

34 HOW DO I USE A
TESTER POT?

Now that you know *why* you need to always buy a tester pot, you should know how to make them useful.

You will need some sheets of plain white printer paper. Paint them all, but leave a border at the bottom so you can write the name of the paint – believe me you will forget, and if you are trying to decide between 15 shades of blush pink (call me thorough) you'll be livid if you haven't noted the name of the best one.

Stick them to the wall and keep looking at them. You must view them in natural and electric light. By the window and in the darkest corner. By the sofa and by the floor. As you narrow them down, paint a second sheet in the favourite and put them next to each other in a corner so you can see how much darker the colour becomes when it goes around a corner and reflects in on itself – some people paint the inside of a shoe box for a similar effect.

35 WHAT COLOUR SHOULD I PAINT THE DOORS AND WINDOWS?

For the most part, I would say paint them to match the walls – that's what the Georgians did and it looks really modern now. Also, if you have chosen a dark wall colour, sometimes white just isn't the best option and can create too much of a contrast, as well as giving the impression that you have outlined the room – like a reverse cartoon.

A long hall with a series of white doors will always look busy and distracting. But a long hall that is a seamless line of the same colour is calmer and will look bigger.

And while we're on doors, remember that they don't have to be painted the same colour on both sides. The rule is that the edge that faces into the room when the door is open is the same colour as the room it is facing into. So usually the handle edge is the colour of the room it is going into and the hinge side is the colour of the room it is facing when open.

36 WHAT ABOUT RADIATORS AND WOODWORK?

Radiators should nearly always be painted to match the walls. And when I say nearly, I mean always. (See Q53 for more advice on what to do about ugly radiators.)

Painting the woodwork the same colour as the walls will make them look taller, which will have the effect of raising the ceiling. It can also make the room look bigger by creating a seamless effect and blurring the boundaries of the space. It looks more modern too.

When you outline the edges of the room in white, you draw attention to them. (And this leads me back to an important point – not all colours go with white. At least not to their best effect; see Q30 for more information –

and for encouragement to not always peg for 'default' white in your scheme.)

Having said that, if you have pale colours on the wall, then a dark window frame or doorway will frame the view rather well. It's up to you if you do the skirtings pale to match the wall or dark to link the door to the window etc.

If you paint a doorframe dark to define and frame the view into the room next door, remember to check that view if you are hanging a picture on the wall – part of a picture will look fine and will lead the eye through the doorway, but if it is a small one that fits fully within the doorframe, it will need to be in the middle or the effect is uncomfortable.

37 WHAT **COLOUR** DO I PAINT THE **CEILING?**

If you have spent lots of money choosing a fabulous colour for the walls, wouldn't it make sense to choose something equally fabulous for the ceiling? Try choosing an actual colour for ceilings rather than just leaving them default white. Dark green walls and pale pink woodwork... Or vice versa (which is what I have in my bedroom). Navy blue walls with a pale pink ceiling... Grey walls with a soft terracotta ceiling... It doesn't have to be white.

You can wallpaper the ceiling to great effect. It's fantastic in a bedroom,

where you're mostly lying down anyway, and if you want to keep the walls pale and neutral then a showstopping ceiling is a great way to add impact that doesn't dominate everything. The ceiling is often referred to as the fifth wall, and once you think of it as such, why not show it off? Particularly if you are hanging a gorgeous pendant light from it. Give it a stunning backdrop.

If you have chosen a pale colour for the walls, then painting the ceiling to match will blur the edges of the space and make it look bigger. If you have a dark colour, then it is a bold step to go dark there as well. It can look superb, but it's not for everyone. If you have a high picture rail, it can look great if the ceiling colour flows down over the edges to meet it. In a room with very high ceilings this will bring things down a bit by making the walls look shorter. This is one of those choice moments. I live in a period house with 8ft high ceilings in narrow rooms. We have chosen to extend the ceiling colour over the walls as we can afford to lose a bit of height visually. Taking a dark colour to the very top of the walls will elongate them, but it will outline the size of the room and can make the overall dimensions appear smaller.

38 WHAT ABOUT FEATURE WALLS?

Feature walls were, ahem, a feature of the 1980s, when it seemed that every room in every house had one random wall that was a different colour from the rest. And therein lay the problem. There's nothing wrong with a feature wall per se – if there is a feature to highlight. But often there isn't. Why is the wall behind the sofa a different colour from the others? It's random and what we are trying to avoid, both in this book and in your house, is random. We are trying to make considered decisions based on answering a number of key questions and the answer is never going to be 'just pick a wall and paint it'.

For the most part, painting one wall a different colour to the others can look like you ran out of paint or didn't have the courage of your convictions when it came to using the feature colour all over. That said, there are exceptions. If you have a wall that is architecturally different – in other words a *genuine* feature wall (rather than one you decided to paint in a different colour because you felt like it) then that can work. It can also be a useful technique to employ if you have a long, narrow room that you want to visually widen; painting the wall at the far end can foreshorten the room and bring that wall closer so it will detract from the narrowness of the space (see Q10).

Another exception is behind the bed. A dramatically coloured wall there can look like a bedhead, so it can be a good idea to match it to that if it's upholstered. The effect will be to make the bed look larger and more luxurious. It's also a great place for wallpaper, as that will show off said bedhead. Painting this wall in a different or dramatic colour will give it impact when you walk into the room, which might make the overall scheme more interesting. And you won't be able to see it when you are in bed, of course, so if it's a strong colour or a bold pattern it won't prevent you from falling asleep.

However, painting the chimney breast in a contrasting colour doesn't really bring anything to the party. That wall already has a feature on it that stands out, so why add another? It also became a design cliché of the last decade and can look a bit dated now. Far better, if you have shelves in an alcove either side of a chimney, to paint, or wallpaper, the backs in a contrasting colour to show off the objects that you might have displayed on them. And I use the word 'objects' advisedly – no point doing that for books, which tend to fill shelves completely.

If you have a chosen colour that you don't want to use on all four walls, then consider the half-painted wall. This is effectively going up to the height of a dado or picture rail (if you have them) in one colour and then painting the wall above, and the ceiling, in a paler colour. If you don't have a dado or picture rail, then just pick a point – somewhere between elbow and shoulder height is good, as ideally you want the contrast to be slightly higher than halfway – and paint across there (see Q39).

That's the best of both worlds: dramatic use of colour that isn't all over. It's worth noting that dark colours tend to look better on the bottom half, but that's not a hard and fast rule.

If you are trying to zone a space, then using different colours of paint can work well, but (a) see if you can paint two walls to create a zoned corner, and (b) consider painting the skirting boards (and doors) of the whole room in the same colour, too. Then the feature wall will become part of the whole, and the room will look more joined up as a result.

There is one wall that can work as a feature wall on its own. It's the fifth wall. Otherwise known as the ceiling (see Q37). I have a gold feature 'wall' in my office. The other four are pale pink.

39 HOW DO YOU **CREATE** A **HALF-PAINTED WALL?**

This is a really good idea if you want to use a strong or dark colour in a room but have (a) read the section about the single feature wall (see Q38) and (b) are nervous about it being 'too much'.

In Victorian houses there is often a dado, or chair, rail that is about halfway up the wall. It's not uncommon to see these walls painted two different shades, or for there to be a combination of wallpaper and paint. Until a few years ago it was considered weird to just paint halfway up a wall with no dado and to then change colour. But times have changed and now it looks both modern and fresh.

In addition, if you paint the bottom half of the wall dark in the living room you can hide the television. If you paint the bottom half of the wall gloss in the hall you can wipe off dirty fingermarks and scuffs from scooters and bicycles.

Of course, the big question is how to achieve a perfectly straight line between the two colours or finishes. I asked Bianca Hall, a serial DIYer and trend expert, for her tips:

Paint the entire wall in your lighter colour, or paint just a bit further than you want your second colour to start. Make sure you feather out the edge so that there are no textured lines, or roller or brush marks where the colour stops.

Next, wait at least 24 hours before you mark with tape where you want the second colour or finish to begin.

For older, fully cured, paint (if you're keeping an existing base colour for example) use green FrogTape. For newer surfaces, use yellow FrogTape.

Mark your line at the desired height. A dado rail height would be around 90cm (35½in) from the floor; a picture rail would be between 30 and 50cm (12 and 20in) from the ceiling. You can use a spirit level, or if you want to go more high-tech, use a laser level.

If you're using a spirit level, decide on your desired line height and, using a tape measure, measure either up from the floor or down from the ceiling, whichever is easiest, marking at intervals just less than your spirit level length across the entire wall. Using your level, work your way along the wall, marking your line across.

The first set of marks are a cross reference to make sure you're on track. If your floor and/or ceiling aren't completely even, you might need to trust your eye more than the spirit level, as a perfectly straight line will look all kinds of wrong and accentuate any wonkiness. In those circumstances, you should go with what looks right, even if it disagrees a little with the spirit level.

If you're using a laser level, you won't need to mark your line with a pencil, just set it up so your laser line is falling in the right place, and you can skip straight to taping.

Use the appropriate painter's tape (green or yellow Frog Tape as previously mentioned) to mask off your line – and to make sure you have a really secure adhesion, run a credit card along the tape with a bit of pressure.

Apply your first coat of paint and allow it to dry according to the manufacturer's instructions. Once you've done your last coat, carefully remove the tape while the paint is still wet to get a clean finish. The same technique can also be used for stripes.

40 WHEN CAN I USE **WALLPAPER** IN THE **BATHROOM?**

When you have good ventilation and a window so you're not turning the room into a giant steam stripper every time you have a shower.

You can also buy waterproof wallpaper these days. Failing that, you can paint over the wallpaper with a coat of Decorators Varnish, which will protect it from splashes and stains. It won't stop the edges curling though so make sure it's glued on really well.

For more advice, you will find a checklist with tips on how to hang wallpaper on the next page.

HOW TO HANG WALLPAPER: A CHECKLIST

CLAIRE GREENFIELD
LEAD DESIGNER AT HARLEQUIN

☐ Prepare the walls. They need to be as smooth as possible, so fill and sand any holes. Apply a weak solution of paste to newly plastered walls and allow it to dry as this helps the paper to stick.

☐ Look at the pattern and find a section that shows the whole design – this is your starting point. It's best to begin on a focal point, such as the chimney breast, if you have one. Otherwise, start in the middle and work towards the corners.

☐ Plan where you will finish, and try and make sure that any difficult pattern match is in a place where it will be the least visible – over the door for example.

☐ Double-check the pattern is the right way up – it doesn't necessarily unroll that way.

☐ Don't be afraid to apply a good layer of paste to the wall as the biggest cause of the edges curling is not using enough. If you get some on the front side of the paper, then wipe immediately with a damp cloth.

☐ Use a spirit level or plumb line to make sure the first length is vertical.

☐ Once a drop is on the wall, there is still time to move it around to match the pattern between sheets. You may need to lift it up to reposition it, but don't be scared of doing this. As long as you have followed the application instructions the paper should move with ease.

☐ Once the paper is on the wall, push it firmly into the ceiling line or skirting board edge and gently score or mark with a pencil. Pull the excess paper back and cut along the line.

☐ After hanging each length, wipe away excess paste with a clean sponge and water, which you must change regularly.

☐ Vinyl wall coverings are a great way to add texture and are good for bathrooms and kitchens as well as high traffic areas. Paper-backed fabrics (laminates) help with acoustics.

WINDOWS & DOORS

41 HOW CAN I MAKE A ROOM LIGHTER?

It's a strange thing that these days we seem to be very comfortable with the idea of moving a wall, or removing it completely. But on moving into a dark house we assume that's that, and all there is to it. Why not see if you can add a window, or a roof light?

Now, there are usually rules about changing the outside appearance of a house, how close a window can be to a neighbour's property, their privacy rights and all that, but sometimes you can add a very high window at the back of your house, or even on a patch of sloping roof so don't rule the idea out. Sloping windows let in twice as much light as vertical ones as they allow light to penetrate further into the room.

So adding windows has to be the first way to make a room lighter. But they don't just have to be outside. Internal windows are a great way of borrowing light from the room next door. You can do this between the hall and the living room, or perhaps from a landing into a dark back bedroom. We borrowed a bit of space from the kitchen to create a downstairs loo under the stairs. I read that blogger Lily Pebbles did the same thing, but with the addition of a really high internal window to bring a little bit of light from the kitchen to that tiny room. It was high and well fitted, so it didn't affect sound or privacy.

If adding windows isn't an option, then you will need to stick to the paler colours on the paint spectrum. But even white paint needs natural light to reflect off it and enable it to do its job of lightening the space. Otherwise it can just look a little drab. So choose a soft white, or a pale green or pink (anything you like as long as it's pale) and then paint the skirting boards, walls, ceiling and doors all the same. This, as I have mentioned previously, will blur the edges and create a calm sense of space.

42 WHAT SORT OF
BLINDS CAN I HAVE?

Roller blinds are the cheapest and easiest style, but many people don't like them in rooms other than kitchens and bathrooms. I have fixed roller blinds across the middle part of my sash windows, where they pretty much disappear until needed.

Roman blinds are the wide slatted ones that pleat up when you raise and lower them. The heavier construction means you can choose velvet for a more luxurious feel, which makes them more appropriate for the living room and bedroom. However, as they fold up on themselves they can take up quite a lot of space at the top of the window and may cut the light. Cheaper mechanisms do have a tendency to go wrong, and then they look messy. If you want this style, then it's best if you can hang them on the wall just above the window frame to avoid losing light.

Venetian blinds are horizontal slats that can be pivoted to let in more or less light. Technically, a genuine Venetian blind is made from metal, and they can be a bit 'office'. Also – they're dust magnets.

Wooden blinds are like Venetians but, er, wooden. They can make a room a lot darker even when the slats are angled open. They can work in kitchens or bathrooms (watch out for grease attracting dust in the former) but aren't really cosy enough for bedrooms and living rooms.

Pleated blinds are a sort of cross between a Roman and a roller. Imagine a very thin Roman blind that rolled right up. Some have a honeycomb shape, which is a great insulator.

Vertical blinds are, as the name suggests, vertical. Like Venetian blinds, these are generally regarded as more office than domestic, although they can work in a 1960s or 1970s period house. I also once saw some made from linen in front of a large French window and the effect was much softer and prettier than the plasticky material they are most commonly made from.

Tie-up blinds are the ones that look like frilly knickers. Two or three cords hang down from the blind that, when pulled, raise the blind, creating a scalloped effect. Best left in the 1980s.

ROLLER BLIND

ROMAN BLIND

TIE-UP BLIND

VENETIAN BLIND

VERTICAL BLIND

PLEATED BLIND

43 HOW MUCH CURTAIN MATERIAL DO I NEED?

Curtains need to be wider than the window if you don't want light to filter through the sides. And to pull properly and appear generous, you need to assume one-and-a-half to two-and-a-half times the width of the window. Decide which you want and multiply it by the length of the curtain pole. Divide the answer by the width of the fabric and round up to the nearest whole number. If your pattern is a large floral that requires matching when the curtains are closed, you'll need more.

You also need to decide what sort of pleating you want across the top. Pencil pleats are the simplest, but you can also have more elaborate pinch pleats. Eyelets are a little old fashioned and tab-tops even more so. Tab-tops can also be harder to pull across a wooden curtain pole, as they don't slide smoothly. Having said that, they allow you to change the curtains easily – the Finns often change their curtains seasonally and choose tab-tops to make that process easier.

44 WHY YOU SHOULDN'T FORGET CURTAIN LININGS

It's a small point, but it is certainly one that's worth considering. Rather than the standard dull beige lining, why not choose a lining in a colour that coordinates with your room or the curtain fabric? A friend of mine has double-sided curtains – one side floral, the other a stripe – on her huge French doors and they look pretty from the outside as well as the inside.

45 WHAT ABOUT FLOOR-LENGTH CURTAINS?

Once upon a time, all houses were draughty. If the window was on the other side of the room from the radiator, the hot air from the radiator would rise, while the cold air from the window would sink and move along the floor, creating a draught. Putting the radiator under the window pushed that cold air upwards where it was warmed by the heat from the radiator, ensuring that any draughts were warm not cold. This is less of a problem now with modern, double-glazed windows, but the question arises: what do you do if you want curtains, as long ones will block the heat from the radiator?

The answer, my friend, is blowing in the draught (as it were). If you can't move the radiators, and short curtains are stylistically wrong, then you need to have blinds that you can pull for privacy during the early part of the evening when the room is being warmed by the radiator. Leave the floor-length curtains open until the room is warm, then you can draw them. The blinds will give some extra insulation too.

46

WHAT ABOUT CURTAINS FOR
AWKWARDLY SHAPED WINDOWS?

The most common culprit is the bay window. Bay windows are big, so they need a lot of curtain. And when that curtain isn't pulled shut it can take up a lot of space on the wall either side – and obscure the light altogether in the two angled side windows.

You can spend a lot of money on a rail that angles right back across the sides of the bay so the curtain goes back across the wall not the window. Bear in mind this will mean you can't have a lamp or a chair in that corner as it will be full of curtain. You can buy curtain rails that fix to the ceiling in front of the window, but the same furnishing issue results. Or you can fix blinds to the windows and have small curtains at the sides that are for decoration only and are never meant to be pulled. It's a compromise, but many things in houses are. If you live in a big house with lots of wall space and big square rooms, this won't be an issue. If you live in a typically narrow Victorian terrace you need all the space you can get, and the curtains aren't helping.

Another common problem is when the window goes right up to the ceiling and there isn't room for a curtain pole. Usually you will have to cheat and fix it either side of the window frame. If that looks odd, add a pelmet. They're not fashionable now, but then nor was grey paint 10 years ago.

British houses are full of oddly shaped windows, from circles to arches and skylights. Sometimes blinds really are the only option. Otherwise you could consider if you really need to cover the window at all.

The trickiest ones I have come across are curved 1930s windows that go around corners. Usually you have to square these off either with curtains or blinds. Alternatively, if you want to keep the shape (and why not – it's a feature) you need to dump the curtain and frost the glass, either with stick-on window film, or something more permanent.

47 WHAT CAN I USE INSTEAD OF NET CURTAINS?

There are various options. You won't like all of them. Pick the one that works for you.

Window film comes in lots of cool patterns and means no one can see in. Unfortunately, you can't see out either.

Voile is sheer material that is very pretty and less naff than nets. For now... But you can also have Roman blinds made from voile, which is a more modern alternative. Consider layering with curtains, as when it's dark outside, people will be able to see in.

Bottom-up blinds do what they say, but you can choose how high you pull them up. This means you can have natural light coming in from the top half of the window, and maintain privacy at the bottom. An alternative to this – which I have done – is to fix a plain roller blind to the middle of the sash window that pulls down to the bottom. It's a cheaper version.

Shutters often have slats that you can angle for privacy. I tend to think they make the room dark all the time but they are insanely popular – even for those who don't live on a plantation.

WHY YOU SHOULD CHANGE THE
DOOR HANDLES
– AND THINK ABOUT HINGES

As with light switches (Q71), handles are details and touch points that you want to get right. Personally, I hate those modern lever handles, as I seem to be incapable of entering a room without catching my clothing and ripping something, but you may be more skilled at walking than me.

There are so many handles you can choose from that it's worth having a good look around. Do you want black, brass or ceramic? Vintage or modern? Round or oval? I would always start by looking at fixtures that fit the period of the building.

Sometimes they didn't always get it right, though. It was the fashion in Victorian times to have doors that opened into rooms so that the people inside had more privacy. But these days that's less of an issue – and also an inward door takes up space in a room when it's open. It can be more space-efficient to swap the hinges, so that it opens against the corner it is closest to, which might just give you more room for a sofa or a chair as a bonus.

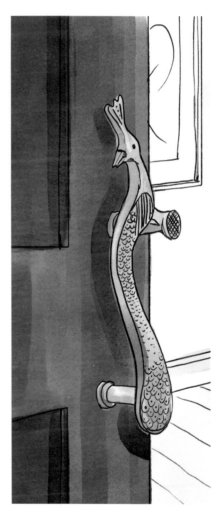

49

WHY YOU SHOULD THINK ABOUT DIFFERENT DOOR STYLES

Fiddling around with doors is something we don't tend to think about. But if you are doing a big refurbishment and you have high ceilings, then think about making the doors taller. Not only will it make you draw yourself up when you enter a space, but it will make the room feel grander and more imposing. And who wouldn't want that? Or you can install a pane of glass above an existing door to bring in more light.

Sometimes it might also be a good idea to cut a door in half to create a folding door, or two small doubles. We did this twice in our house instead of installing a sliding door. At the top of the first flight of stairs is a very small shower room. There was nowhere for a sliding door to slide to, so that wasn't an option. But there was a real risk that if one child flung open the door

when coming out of that room they could hit the other one coming up the stairs. The solution was to ask the builder to cut the door in half and put hinges down the middle so the door folds back on itself when open and takes up half as much room.

When we were knocking through from our bedroom to the one next door to create an en suite bathroom we had a similar issue. A full-sized door would have taken up too much space when opened into whichever room we chose it to swing into. This time we decided to cut the door in half and attach one section to each side of the frame. That way it is a narrow double door that doesn't dominate the rooms either side. The moral of the story is that you don't have to accept the doors you have. There are better ways to make them fit your house and your life.

50
WHEN IS A
SLIDING DOOR USEFUL?

It's basically a giant space saver. We had a tiny utility room in the corner of our kitchen for years and we were always frustrated by how small it was. One day we realized that we had lost a whole wall of potential storage to the

door opening against it. We changed it to a sliding door – which involved moving the washing machine by a couple of inches – but suddenly we had created masses more storage space.

If you have a bit of wall where the door can slide to then it's worth considering for cupboards, downstairs loos, pantries, wardrobes, rooms off narrow corridors etc. We put a sliding door on the bathroom in our loft as, because of the sloping ceiling, it would have had to open outwards otherwise, which would have been dangerous to anyone coming up the stairs into the main room. I bought a rustic-looking wrought iron sliding mechanism from eBay and got our builders to fashion the door itself from leftover floorboards. It wouldn't work for a bathroom in the middle of the house, but for one that functions only as either an office loo or an en suite when the loft is used as a spare room, it's private enough.

Pocket doors are more expensive, but more modern than the barn door idea above. A pocket door slides between two walls – one of which is false, so that it disappears completely when open. It looks sleeker and tidier than the sliding barn door idea. But you can probably DIY the latter, whereas you will need a specialist fitter for the former.

STANDARD MEASUREMENTS: A CHECKLIST

☐ A standard door is 1981mm (78in) high and varies in width, but 762mm (30in) is the most common in England and Wales, with 838mm (33in) for wheelchairs.

☐ A kitchen cupboard is usually 60cm (23½in) wide and deep, but Ikea makes 40cm (16in) and 20cm (8in) variants. You can, of course, go bespoke, but knowing this will give you a rough idea of how much storage you can fit in at a glance.

☐ A standard single mattress is 91 x 190cm (36 x 75in); a standard double mattress is 137 x 190cm (54 x 75in); and a standard king-size mattress is 152 x 198cm (60 x 78in).

☐ A bath is usually 1700 x 700mm (67 x 27½in), and a short one tends to be 1500mm (59in) long but the same width (700mm/27½in). A large one is 1800 x 800mm (71 x 31½in).

☐ Generally speaking there are 13 stairs in a flight. After 16 you must have a landing. When calculating carpet, it is roughly 25cm (10in) for the step and 20cm (8in) for the riser, making a total of around 45cm (18in) per stair. You need to multiply that by the width of the stair. This is for a straight flight.

☐ Ideally you would have 750mm (29½in) from the front of the loo to a wall or shower screen to allow comfortable seating. This can be reduced in a downstairs loo if the basin is there as knees can fit under.

☐ A shower cubicle should be a minimum of 800 x 800mm (31½ x 31½in) so as not to feel cramped.

☐ When planning shelves it's useful to know that a standard paperback book is 23 x 13cm (9 x 5in), *Elle Decoration* is 285 x 220mm (11¼ x 8½in) and an office ring binder is 31.5 x 24.5cm (12½ x 9¾in). Don't forget to factor in the thickness of the wood for the shelf itself.

FIXTURES & FURNISHINGS

51 WHAT DO I **SPEND** THE **MOST ON?**

We spend a third of our lives in bed, so it may not be the most exciting answer but I think a good mattress is really worth the investment. After that it's a sliding scale, but the basic rule of thumb is that you should always buy the best you can afford.

Designer kitchen labels can help with resale, and a good quality sofa will last you for years. An accent chair that isn't going to be sat on that often (or is the bedroom chairdrobe) doesn't need to cost a fortune.

So think carefully about what you want and how long you need it to last. If you think you might be moving house then it's probably not worth spending a lot of money on a really good sofa or curtains, as the chances are it/they won't fit in the new place. A mattress is a standard size though, so you won't go wrong with that.

52 WHY YOU SHOULD
MAKE FRIENDS
WITH A CARPENTER

Good carpentry is expensive, but it makes a huge difference to a house. We have a library and our carpenter made the shelves out of MDF in about two days. They took nearly a week to paint, mind, but they are one of best features of the house. A good carpenter will knock you up some shelves, build you a cupboard, come up with a plan to hide the TV and help you manage the storage under the stairs from a drawing you made on the back of an envelope. Ready-made shelves will never fit a space as well, and still need fixing to the wall anyway.

Thanks to our carpenter, we have a tiny little shelf next to the washing machine that stores a bucket with all the cleaning stuff. As it's next to the washing machine there was nothing to fix it to, so it is suspended from the shelf above by a couple of upside-down metal brackets. It's not pretty, but it is useful and it only took about an hour. It would have taken my husband a whole morning and cost a divorce. The right person for the job will have the right tools and a better way of doing it.

To make matters more economical, you can always make a list of everything you want doing and get it done in one go. A sheet of MDF is very affordable and it's big, so you can do a lot with it. And don't forget that fitted storage is 30 per cent more efficient than freestanding. So, it's definitely worth finding a bit more in the budget to have something made to measure.

53 WHAT CAN I DO ABOUT UGLY RADIATORS?

It's a fact that most radiators aren't things of beauty. Yet we draw attention to their presence by leaving them like white beacons on our freshly papered and painted walls. So the first thing I am going to say is: paint them. Always paint them to match the wall so they disappear. And if you have wallpaper then pick one of the colours in that, so it looks like you made a decision.

Now, full disclosure, I said this at a talk once and was told off by a plumber who said it would affect the heat given out. You can take advice on that. Mine are painted and I haven't noticed any difference in temperature or efficiency.

If painting isn't an option, then maybe you need to replace them altogether. Old school-style radiators are fashionable (and pricey) and can be sprayed to match your walls. Or, if you have spent a lot of money on them and they are attractive in themselves, consider a contrasting colour. Who says you can't have a radiator that tones with the cushions? After all, if you've spent money making it a feature of the room then allow it to stand out. Treat it like another piece of furniture, which it sort of is. Just a fixed one.

54 WHAT DO I NEED TO KNOW ABOUT INSTALLING A WOOD -BURNING STOVE?

Our kitchen is north facing. It is practically Baltic in the winter and the two radiators in there just don't seem to make any difference. We had long fantasized about installing a wood-burner – and I had spent many winters wearing scarves and fingerless gloves while typing away at the kitchen table like a character in a Dickens novel. Two years ago, we took the plunge and installed a wood-burning stove. And then at precisely the same moment, there was a rash of headlines about how wood-burning stoves were going to be banned, how they were massively anti-environment, how only the terrible metropolitan elite middle classes have them, and how generally awful they were (both the middle classes and the stoves). 'Well,' I said to The Mad Husband, 'It looks amazing – maybe we just won't light it.' But we wanted to and we have. So here are the things you need to know.

Around 10 per cent of UK homes have an open fire or a wood-burning stove and, according to a BBC report, pollution from burning wood and coal in the home currently causes 38 per cent of particulate pollution – far outweighing that caused by industrial combustion (16 per cent) and road transport (12 per cent). In 2018 the UK government announced that it was proposing to phase out the sale of wet wood and coal for domestic use; those bags you pick up at the garage or the DIY store are not only the most expensive way to buy, but often contain wet logs which are vastly more polluting than seasoned (dry) wood, as they give off so much more smoke.

Wood-burning stoves won't be banned, but since 2019 you are only allowed to burn dry wood or smokeless fuels in them. Basically, coal is a no-no. Instead you want dry, seasoned wood with a moisture content of less than 20 per cent, or a smokeless solid fuel such as anthracite. (A list of approved fuels is available on the Solid Fuels Association website.) You can buy a moisture meter to check your wood. And you will also need to buy a stove that has been approved for use in smoke-controlled areas by Defra, or a clean-burning 'ecodesign ready' model that conforms to EU regulations coming in in 2022, as well as stricter North American low emission levels. Ecodesign is the European-wide programme to lower emissions.

You can install a wood-burning stove in your fireplace, but you need to bear in mind that a wood-burning stove requires a narrower flue than an open fire, so you can't just rip out the fireplace, stick in a stove and point it up the chimney. You will have to install the correct flue. And if you don't have a chimney, then any member of a Competent Person Scheme (someone who is officially registered to carry out this type of work) will be able to advise you on this. You will need to have the chimney flue placed on the exterior of the house, and it must be insulated to work properly.

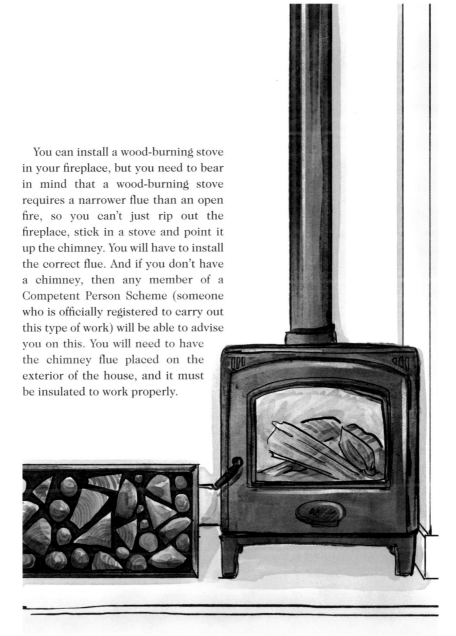

55 WHEN TO **SPLURGE** AND WHEN TO **SAVE** ON **FURNITURE**

Generally speaking it's hard to advise on this as one person's dream piece will be another's nightmare. I was asked to design a shop selling high-end fashion for a women's charity. I was thrilled to acquire a light made from a dress mannequin sprayed gold with a lampshade made out of feathers that resembled a hat. When I asked the builder to move a socket so I could plug it in in the right place, he muttered that if his wife had brought home something similar he would certainly have refused to let it in the house and possibly divorced her as well. But if you fall in love with something totally impractical that you are going to love for ever then trust your gut. I still love my 6ft tall, brass palm tree lamp, and while not an obviously sensible purchase, I maintain it was necessary.

That said, it's always worth buying the best appliances you can afford. Invest in anything with moving parts – taps, handles, and light switches – as well as pieces where you spend a lot of time – beds and sofas. Occasional armchairs can be more statement than comfort and occasional tables more trend than investment. It's a bit like the old cost per wear equation that we all use to justify an expensive piece of clothing. If you are going to use it every day then it's worth spending money on. If it's for the dining room or the spare room, or only going to be used at Christmas and every other Sunday, then less so.

56 WHAT PIECE OF **FURNITURE** DO I BUY **FIRST?**

The usual answer to this question seems to be a bed, but I would narrow that down to a mattress. We had been together for five years before we stopped sleeping on a mattress on the floor. When we did eventually graduate to a bed it was a very budget-friendly metal one from Ikea. Once you have sorted your sleeping arrangements, buy a sofa.

57

HOW DO I
MIX DIFFERENT
WOODS?

This is often unavoidable. If you have a wooden floor the chances are that you will have a wooden table too. There are ways around it though – rugs can break up a fight, for example. If both floor and table are in matching wood then try contrasting the chairs – painted wood (see Q60), plastic or metal will separate everything and create a contemporary look. Try looking for a table with metal legs if you don't want a rug under it, as this will also put distance between tabletop and floor.

Furniture tends to look better if it's at least from a similar period or is a similar colour. I have an antique mahogany desk with a vintage pine dresser in my office. The colours – both warm – work together. If you have a wooden floor then that has to be the starting point as it's the biggest thing in the room. Decide first if that has warm or cool tones. That will be the guide to choosing the rest of the wood in the room.

On that basis, it may be best to go with a contrast as it can be hard to match pieces unless you're buying a set, which you aren't – as I said in the first book (what do you mean you haven't got it?), you want to give the impression that you've thought about your furniture and not just loaded a matching set into your cart (virtual or otherwise). So, for instance, you could have a dark floor, light table and contrasting chairs, and if all the elements are wood, you're going to need a rug.

Ultimately it will come down to your eye, and if you are nervous then it's best to try and avoid mixing them completely. Instead you should choose a glass table, painted wood or coloured plastic chairs.

58 WHAT ARE GOOD INVESTMENT BUYS?

It's not just about buying a good quality mattress or a well-made sofa, sometimes we want to invest in a piece of antique furniture that will look wonderful, add character and can be passed down through the family – a great clock or a fantastic Persian rug, for example. These purchases can be expensive and you don't want to get it wrong, so I asked Philippa Curphey...

PHILIPPA CURPHEY
STYLIST

The interiors world is experiencing a cross-collecting revolution and I am a very big fan of filling clients' homes with different moments of history which are rich in provenance and heritage to complement their existing pieces.

When sourcing an antique, I would advise people to not just think about its long-term monetary value, but consider acquiring a one-off piece that is personal to them. It could be an original piece of art that triggers an experience they have had, or an antique chair that comes with its own unique story – this is far more valuable, in my opinion, than its financial worth.

Whether you're buying a French oil painting, an industrial statement light or an art deco mirror, it's important to consider how your antique piece will sit alongside your existing furniture. Think about space and visual impact – less is certainly more – and to avoid turning your house into an antiques jumble, I would recommend sourcing a few larger statement pieces. Above all, be brave, be bold and keep it personal to get maximum visual impact within the space. For more advice see Q62.

CONTEMPORARY AND PERIOD FURNITURE?

This is all about the red thread. Put simply, you can mix different periods, although some will go better than others, but you need a link between them all – and that is the red thread. The concept is derived from Greek mythology (Theseus found his way out of the Minotaur's labyrinth by following a red thread given to him by Ariadne), and it's a principle that has been used in many different contexts ever since.

I came across the idea when talking to a designer with the Danish company BoConcept, who claimed it as a Nordic design philosophy, since it's a common metaphor in Scandinavia and used to illustrate a shared characteristic that runs through connecting themes, stories, ideas and interior design.

Let's start with the basics. You can always put modern furniture in a period house and vice versa. I've lost count of the times I've seen an amazing modern glass house on Grand Designs and thought the interiors would be much improved with some Persian rugs and antique furniture to bring character and add personality to the space. Georgian and Victorian houses, on the other hand, with their ornate panelling, coving and cornicing, respond well to the clean lines of mid-century modern furniture.

But no one has all of everything and sometimes you need to know how to mix it up a little more. So you've got your grandmother's antique bureau that you don't want to part with, but you need a new coffee table and sofa and you wouldn't mind some more storage while you're at it. Sound familiar? If you need to create a mix of periods you need to have a common element that brings the room – with all its disparate furniture styles – together. And that is the red thread.

For instance, mix woods but make sure they are of the same tone (see Q57). If you have a modern marble coffee table, you might want to put a marble clock on top of the antique desk in the corner. If your table has black metal legs then consider a couple of black candlesticks on the sideboard.

You might want black shelves on the wall that echo those black legs. Or perhaps you have an old wooden candlestick that can go on the modern shelving unit.

When it comes to the sofa and chairs, try to make sure the shapes work together. The delicate legs and carving of a French antique table won't work with a huge, square, modular sofa. Try to pick a sofa on taller legs (a little more mid-century in style) or with narrow arms, so the two pieces can have a relationship of equals – plus thin arms mean you get more space to sit.

Years ago (and I mean years) I worked in a clothing shop in Paris which sold jeans and leather jackets and shirts in quite a chichi area of the city. I have never forgotten a very elegant French woman, of a certain age, who came in and bought three pairs of jeans – and different socks to co-ordinate with each one. I was astounded. But then that's the French way of dressing. And it's not a bad idea for us. Once you start to look at the room like this – as a whole, rather than as a collection of disparate elements – it comes together more easily. When you buy a new piece of clothing you should always think about what you already have that it will go with. Some say that if you can't think of three outfits to put it with then you shouldn't buy it. That might be quite extreme, but the point is that you should be thinking of your wardrobe as a whole. It's the same with your room.

So don't buy the coffee table or the sofa in isolation but think about what you already have. And if a couple of accessories that go with the new table can sit on or near something else to tie the scheme together, then you should buy them as well. And while we're on the subject, it's not just about the whole room. In an open-plan space, or a room with a direct view from the one you are in, you need to carry the thread through there to link the two. You need to think of the whole house to keep the scheme cohesive. That red thread? It worked for Theseus.

60 WHEN IS IT OK TO
PAINT FURNITURE?

I used to think that the answer to this was never. Too many shabby-chic dressing tables and badly painted farmhouse tables had left me feeling more distressed than the furniture. But then someone pointed out that some high-end designer furniture is often just painted MDF. I also interviewed Annie Sloan, the queen of chalk paint, about her rules for painting furniture and I started to think that perhaps it isn't always such a bad idea.

Having said that, let's get one thing out of the way. Don't paint it and then scrape it off again. Paint it and paint it well and then varnish or seal it over the top so it looks good and the colour is properly saturated. This will look way more expensive than the shabby chic side of things.

Right, that said, what can we paint? I'm going to say no to the antiques. If you have a properly old piece of furniture that is causing you distress then try selling it and use the money to buy something more suitable. A lot of old furniture isn't antique and isn't worth anything, so go for it. I might

baulk at painting mahogany but there's no shortage of antique pine and since it tends to go a rather unattractive orange with age, by all means stick some colour on it. I think it's fine to paint reproduction antiques as well. They're just old-fashioned copies of an original, after all. Remember that you don't have to stick to painting wood – MDF and chipboard take paint perfectly well and you will be able to inject personality into a generic piece.

What about Ikea furniture? There is a period in life – in your late 20s to early 30s – when you start to think that instead of spending all your salary on beer you might buy a cushion, or a table for your house. Most of us start off in Ikea because it's affordable. But you can make items look much more expensive – not to mention more individual. One word: paint. That way you are creating something bespoke out of something mass-produced – which has got to be a good idea.

If you are buying something specifically to paint it, then put a cap on your spending so you don't go mad.

61 WHY SHOULD I BUY OLD OR VINTAGE ITEMS?

Firstly, buying a vintage piece is saving it from landfill. It's the sustainable and green option. Whether it's adding to a collection of retro cake-stands or reupholstering an old chair, a vintage piece can be cheaper and also a good investment.

And consider this. Vintage chairs are often very comfortable as they were well made and built to last, while old chests of drawers often have much deeper drawers than their modern counterparts. They are also made from solid wood rather than chipboard and veneer, with dovetailed joints on drawer corners instead of glue and screws. They are quality pieces.

It's not just that. Buying vintage also means you can create a more individual look. The rise in the popularity of flatpack furniture meant that there was a point during the nineties when you could go out for a drink with your mates and wonder whose house you were in if you fell asleep on the sofa

and woke up an hour later. But buying vintage pieces brings a rich layer of history, character and personality into your home.

While it may have a scratch or a mark from years gone by, period furniture has stories to tell. Our old kitchen table came from an art school and I loved the inkblots and scratches and liked to imagine what had been created by people who sat there before us.

Vintage furniture will have a patina to it that modern pieces cannot replicate. Brown furniture is also staging a comeback. For years it has been out in the wilderness while we bought modern and contemporary and often cheap chipboard. But it's coming back and that's a good thing.

You can still find cheap old furniture that isn't worth anything financially but this is perfect to upcycle. Wallpaper the drawers, add a leather top, reupholster or paint it (see Q60). Make it your own completely bespoke piece.

62

WHAT ABOUT
ANTIQUE FURNITURE?

Antiques sit happily next to more modern pieces (see Q59) and will work well in both contemporary and cottage environments. But just as I wouldn't suggest buying all modern, nor would I propose filling your whole house with antiques.

For more advice I went back to stylist and design expert Philippa Curphey.

PHILIPPA
CURPHEY
STYLIST

Do your research: Before venturing into the antiques buying world, spend some time doing your research at antique fairs, flea markets and auctions. They are the places to get inspired, discover new trends and rediscover old ones. It's also a great opportunity to set up a platform to meet reputable dealers, learn from the experts and build relationships with the professionals, who will be more than happy to share their wealth of knowledge with you.

Know what to look for: When looking for a genuine antique piece of furniture, my rule of thumb is to always look closely at how it has been made. An antique shouldn't have that feel of being mass-produced. The quality of the construction and craftsmanship should be of a high level, with slight handmade imperfections. The piece should be solid and heavy to lift, yet look authentically aged in its appearance. Reputable dealers should also provide you with a receipt when purchasing, so be sure to ask for one for that added reassurance. There are several books, magazines, antiques guides and online resources out there that will help educate you on how to avoid being ripped off by 'dodgy dealers'. Miller's antiques guides are good investments, while *Homes & Antiques* magazine and *Antiques Trade Gazette* are other publications worth signing up to.

Always be Prepared: You need a tape measure, porter's trolley and packing material to make your life easier and to avoid any mistakes or accidents. Cash is also very important if you want to barter for a bargain. Most sellers mark their prices up in preparation for a good barter so just go for it and start LOW. It is also worth hanging around until the dealers are about to leave to make that cheeky offer, as they will usually want to shift their stock at the end of the event to avoid lugging anything back on their vans.

HOW TO ADD CHARACTER TO A NEW BUILD: A CHECKLIST

☐ Don't be tempted to add antique features like panelling to a modern room – it will always look fake and ersatz. Use paint in more interesting ways inside, such as coloured woodwork, half-painted walls, even diagonals.

☐ If the ceilings are low and you want to add colour then try painting halfway up the walls in a strong colour and using a pale colour on the top half and over the ceiling (see Q37, Q38 and Q39 for more advice). You can also use the same colour but put gloss on the bottom and matt on the top.

☐ If it's full of downlights in a grid, get an electrician to remove and rearrange to suit your furniture layout and what you are using the spaces for (see Q70).

☐ If bedroom ceilings are too low for a single central pendant, then think about hanging one on either side of the bed as a bedside light, which will free up space on a bedside table – if there is room for one. Or perhaps hang a pendant in a corner to make a feature.

☐ A bit of vintage furniture will go a long way towards adding character to a new build, so go to junk shops and scour eBay for old pieces (see Q61). A fabulous antique dresser can look amazing against a plain white wall.

☐ Mid-century furniture always looks good, and the clean lines and heritage feel work well in modern box-type rooms.

☐ If there is the option to replace carpets with floorboards downstairs, then take it. And add rugs on the boards to bring in colour and personality.

☐ New-build houses tend to be fairly featureless, so you need to fill them with things to make them look inviting and warm. Books are your friends – nothing furnishes a room like a bookshelf – and hang lots of pictures on the wall.

☐ Think about painting the woodwork and doors in a strong colour to add character – this works if you prefer to keep the walls pale.

☐ It's vital that not everything matches – you cannot have a three-piece suite in a new build if you want it to have personality. Pick a great sofa and a couple of armchairs in different styles, but match the tones. Bring in lots of different but natural textures – wool, velvet, linen and old wood. If the vintage isn't in the fabric of the building then bring it via the furnishings.

LIGHTING

63 WATT THE LED IS A LUMEN?

It doesn't matter how many light bulbs you currently have in your house – I have three boxes of the damn things – it is a truth universally acknowledged that you haven't got one to fit that light that just blew. And if, by some miracle, you do have one that fits the socket, the chances are it won't be the right wattage. Perhaps it's an LED (light emitting diode) rather than an incandescent tungsten bulb. In which case you need to look at the number of kelvins to get the right atmosphere.

What does it all mean? Why can't I just go to bed and read my book? I've got a torch. Even a candle will do. And actually you can get battery-operated candles now, so maybe that's the answer. Well pay attention, because this will explain all. And while I would never advocate tearing books up – certainly mine – this might be a page that you want to at least photograph and keep handy.

First, a note on fittings. The bayonet is mostly a UK thing and they are being phased out in favour of screw fittings – known as the Edison Screw Cap or E for short and named after their inventor, Thomas Edison. And E27 is the wider one that corresponds to a standard bayonet fitting – the 27 corresponds to the size in mm. So you will also find E14 in smaller lamps.

Now the different types of bulbs:

TUNGSTEN refers to the old incandescent bulbs that work by heating a filament with electricity until it becomes white-hot and glows. Put like that, it sounds extraordinarily dangerous doesn't it? While cheap to make, they are poor at energy efficiency as only about 5 per cent of the energy they use is converted into visible light.

HALOGEN lights are the closest to incandescent bulbs in terms of light quality. The filament is enclosed in halogen gas so they can burn hotter than an incandescent, but will use up to 30 per cent less energy. They are much cheaper than the LEDs and CFLs (read on). Halogens reach full brightness straight away and don't have to warm up like some CFLs. They can be used with dimmer switches. They will give you a warm light but won't last as long as other energy saving bulbs – around two years.

CFL (compact fluorescent lamp) bulbs are the most common bulbs and are the original alternative to the incandescent bulbs, using between 60 and 80 per cent less energy. They don't

have a filament, but create light by using an electric current to excite gases within the bulb that causes a phosphorous coating on the inside of the bulb to glow, creating light. But they can take time to warm up so aren't great for bathrooms, for example, where you might want instant brightness. They also contain a small amount of mercury, so should always be properly recycled. They don't always work with dimmers and often come in unusual shapes – so they can stick out of the lampshade that goes with the stand, making the whole thing awkward. However, they are more energy efficient than halogens and give off a warm, soft light, even if they do look unattractive when switched off.

LED (light emitting diodes) bulbs use very little energy and can last for more than 20 years, but they can be expensive. Rather than heating a filament, LEDs produce light through a semi-conductor that emits light energy when an electrical current passes through it. They consume 90 per cent less energy than a tungsten bulb and will, over time, bring your bills down. But they don't always work with dimmers and some have a cooler bluish light. Annoyingly this will vary between manufacturers, making it hard to achieve a consistent look in your house if you are replacing bulbs over time to save on costs. It can be worth buying one to check you like it before you splash out on the whole house.

So that's the fittings and the bulbs dealt with. What about the actual light? Before the arrival of energy saving bulbs, a watt was an easy way of working out how much light you were going to get. So 40W was a dim, ambient glow that wasn't going to get that needle threaded, while 100W was perfect for working and reading. But the arrival of LEDs meant it was no longer possible to judge by numbers alone. A 10W LED might be much brighter than a 40W bulb. And that is where the confusion starts.

The issue is that a watt measures how much power the bulb has, which is not the same as how much light it gives out. And that, my friends, is what the lumen does – it tells you the measurement of light visible to the eye from a light source.

Now all you need to do is establish what kind of bulb you are replacing and look at the chart below to compare watts and lumens.

Now, it's not quite over yet because if you have LEDs you have to make another decision between warm or cold light, and this is measured in kelvins. The higher the kelvin the cooler the light. So, put simply, you might want a warm light in the living room and a cooler one in the kitchen. A candle is about 1,500K, a standard warm white (like a traditional incandescent bulb) is about 2,700K, a natural white is around 3,000, and a cool white – which might start to look a little clinical – is around 4000K. Hit 5000K and it starts to look like you're performing an autopsy rather than baking a cake.

So now you know all that, how do you buy the right bulb? Well, roughly speaking, you want about 400 lumens for a bedside light and a total of between 1,500 and 3,000 in a living room once you've added up the different sources from all the lamps in the room.

HOW MANY LUMENS DO YOU NEED? (240V)

BRIGHTNESS	220+	400+	700+	900+	1300+
TUNGSTEN	25W	40W	60W	75W	100W
HALOGEN	18W	28W	42W	53W	70W
CFL	6W	9W	12W	15W	20W
LED	4W	8W	10W	13W	18W

64
HOW MUCH
LIGHT DO I NEED?

These days we are all aware of the role good lighting plays in our homes as a way of decorating the space and showing off artwork and objects, but it's important to remember its primary function as a tool to help us see properly without straining our eyes. As a general rule, all rooms should have layers of light – this means that you should include overhead, floor and task lamps. Wall lights are good for highlighting pictures or creating an ambience by washing light gently up and down, but aren't essential. Dimmer switches, however, are.

Lighting a room doesn't end there. You need to make sure that your lighting scheme is fit for purpose. You can keep the general lighting low as long as you make sure that what you want to read, knit or sew is well lit.

This means a table lamp by the chair or a floor lamp at the end of the sofa. Don't panic that you must have a super bright 100W bulb, but do make sure that if you have a 40W bulb, it is quite close to whatever you are doing. Angled lamps are excellent for this, and remember: a dark shade will focus the light directly up and down, while a pale one will diffuse it gently all round.

When you are sitting at a computer, you need to ensure that you are about an arm's length away from the top of the screen and that it is positioned so you are always looking downwards. Keep the brightness similar to your surroundings to minimize strain. Make sure that angled lights are shining on what it is you are doing, even if the rest of the room is plunged into a Dickensian gloom.

65

HOW TO CREATE
ATMOSPHERE
WITH LIGHTING

When you have arranged your ceiling lights you will then need to think about positioning the other lights in the room. And you will need different lights at different heights to create atmosphere – and let's not forget, to let you see what you are doing.

A floor light is good in a corner. It works well next to a sofa, so you can cast light down onto what you are doing. It also, obviously, creates a higher pool of light and can show off a picture on the wall. Talking of artwork, modern picture lights are a good way to add a little ambient lighting to a room. You can find some that can be painted to match the wall so the item itself disappears, leaving (rather like the Cheshire Cat and its grin) simply the light it is giving out.

Consider if you want to wash light up a wall or down a curtain, and choose the shape accordingly. Don't forget that a dark lampshade will throw light only up or down and not create an ambient glow around the edges. That's the same with all those fashionable metal lamps that are around at the moment. They look great when they're turned off but you can't see a damn thing when they're on.

Finally, you need a mix of task and table lamps. The former for reading, the latter for creating atmosphere when you're watching TV or drinking wine. Or both. Try to have them at different heights. If it's a pain to turn them all on and off you can have them wired to a central switch, or two, so you can turn them on at the wall when you enter the room. We have some of ours on timers, but you do have to change the hours quite often as the daylight waxes and wanes.

66 HOW CAN I FIT A CHANDELIER IN THE BATHROOM?

The first thing you really need to know when tackling bathroom lighting is that the room is zoned according to the distance between the water and the light fitting. Zone 0 is basically in the bath and on the floor of the shower. Zone 1 is within the shower enclosure or directly behind the bath. Zone 2 stretches for 600mm (23½in) either side of the outside of the shower and the ends of the bath. If you want a chandelier over the bath it needs to be 1.5m (5ft) from the top of the water when the bath is filled, or, in other words, you need a ceiling of around 2.25m high – nearly eight feet. This basically rules out a pendant over the

bath for most of us, but you might be able to have one in a different zone so that it's not hanging over the water – the middle of the room for example, if the bath is to one side. Or perhaps hanging in a corner, creating a feature that is well away from the bath.

But if you can't have a statement pendant in the bathroom, then consider wall lights. These will reflect on to the water in the bath and create a gorgeous shimmering light that will be really atmospheric. The other key thing you really need to know when choosing lighting for the bathroom (and to a certain extent the kitchen) is the IP rating...

67 WHAT IS AN
IP RATING?

IP stands for Ingress Protection and means how well a light fitting is sealed against dust, contact, and, in the case of bathrooms, water. We have looked at the zones (see Q66) but when you are buying bathroom lights, you must also check the IP rating. Some wall lights won't be suitable for bathrooms at all. Generally speaking, outside lights will be fine.

There are usually two important numbers: the first is general intrusion protection, the second relates to water.

A bathroom light should generally be IP65, which means protected against dust that may harm the equipment inside, and protected against low-pressure water jets from all directions. You will also often see IP44, which means it is protected from solid objects greater than 1mm – so not dust but small tools and wires – and against water splashing from all directions. You'll find IP tables online, and you should check if the fittings you like would be allowed.

Based on @sophierobinsoninteriors

68 WHEN SHOULD I GET RID OF THE PENDANT LIGHT?

When it's hanging pointlessly down from the middle of the room but there's nothing there for it to light apart from a patch of bare floor. This is often the case in bedrooms where the pendant ends up somewhere near the end of the bed. In the living room it's often slightly off-centre of the coffee table or at one end of the dining table. It doesn't have to be that way.

First of all, have a think about where it might be most useful. Then have a think about where it might look most amazing. Pendant lights come in for a lot of bad press – it's more fashionable to have ambient lighting dotted around the room. But sometimes you just want to flick a switch by the door so you can see your way to the aforementioned ambient lighting, and that means the pendant doesn't have to be in the middle of the room.

What about hanging a dramatic light in the corner of the room? That works as a piece of art, instead of a picture. It also frees up floor space, which will make the room look bigger. I once advised a chess-loving client, who liked to have a game permanently set up, to hang a pendant light low over his chess table in the corner. Once you have decided where it would look good and work well, you have two options. One is to move it permanently to that spot, which will involve the electrician, possibly the plasterer and the painter as the light will need to be moved, the plaster chased out to bury the wire and then it will all need to be painted. Or you can buy a length of coloured electrical flex and a cup hook. Ask the electrician to rewire the light then drape it across the ceiling from the central rose to the cup hook and let it hang down from there. This has the advantage of allowing you to move it to another space with another hook or return it to the centre if you loop up the excess cable.

Now you have a pendant light that is a feature in its own right, doubles up as ambient light and you can see where you're going as soon as you're in the room – which if you watch any thrillers is a good idea, as the villain is always sitting in the best armchair in the dark.

69 HOW LOW SHOULD I HANG A PENDANT LIGHT OVER A TABLE?

Most people keep them too high and they sort of hover by the ceiling looking a bit like a guest that's hanging back on the edge of a conversation, never quite sure when they can break in. If you are going to have pendant lights over the table then they need to be low enough to be part of the scene.

Generally speaking, they should be slightly higher than the tallest person's head when they are sitting down. Go about 15cm (6in) higher so the light from the bulb won't dazzle, and they will also be able to have a conversation with the person sitting opposite them. If you think this will be too low in the event of the table being moved for a party (and how often is this likely to happen?) you can keep the lights on a long flex and simply loop and knot the flex to the right height when the table is underneath (see Q68). Attach some cup hooks to the ceiling or the wall and then, when you move the table for dancing, you can hang the lights over the hooks and out of the way.

70 HOW DO I **ARRANGE DOWNLIGHTS?**

You need to layer the lights in your room so that you have different types for different jobs and to create different atmospheres. But before you can work any of that out, you need to start with a furniture plan, as it's only when you have arranged the furniture that you can see where the lights should go.

I tend to use downlights only in kitchens and bathrooms, but they can work well in other rooms if you arrange them correctly. First, resist the temptation to arrange them in a symmetrical grid. They will be tidy on the ceiling but inevitably in the wrong places for what is happening below. Also, you shouldn't be looking at the ceiling anyway, but be merely aware of the fact that there is enough light coming from that direction to see what you're doing. In the kitchen, put lights over the work surfaces but make sure they are in front of where your head will be when you stand there so they don't cast a shadow. In a bathroom, do the same thing in front of the mirrors.

It's in the living room that the furniture plan is key. To start with, this is a room that should mainly be lit by ambient lamps, but a few spotlights around the edges can also create atmosphere, if they're on a dimmer. Set them about 30–40cm (12–16in) in from the edge of the ceiling, where

they can wash light down the front of a bookshelf for example. Rather than putting one in the middle of the ceiling (where it might be a bit pointless like the aforementioned pendant, see Q68), place them above the centres of the windows – that way they will cast a pretty arc of light over the curtains or blinds at night. And there's no need to put one over the TV in the corner, as that's best left dark. Those are the lights that work with the structure of the room, although it can also be pretty to have one that falls over the middle of the coffee table.

You can aim for the same arrangement in the bedroom – around the edges and the middle of the windows. That way you won't have one shining in your eyes when you're lying in bed reading. Remember that the furniture plan is important, because if you're having downlights installed, it's likely you will also want to install or move sockets at the same time so you can arrange the lamps you need.

Downlights must be on a dimmer and, particularly in a kitchen-diner and bathroom, it can be worth having them on different circuits, so that you can turn off the kitchen ones when you're sitting at the table, or just keep the lights on over the basins when you're lying in the bath.

WHY SHOULD I **SWITCH** MY (PLASTIC) **SWITCHES?**

There's no point arguing about it, those white plastic switches are ugly and they're not particularly tactile either. The details and touch points in any building are the bits that we interact with, so we should make them more pleasurable to use and make sure they look good at the same time.

These days there is a mass of choice for switches, so do explore the options. You can get white metallic ones if you want them to disappear, brass or copper if you want to match them to door and window handles, black industrial ones or even Perspex ones that disappear and are good for wallpapered walls.

Toggle switches make a pleasing click and are nice to use, too, so you are more likely to turn the lights off when you leave a room.

The devil is in the detail, as they say.

LIGHTING: A CHECKLIST

☐ If you are starting the room from scratch then you must make a furniture plan first. That way you can work out where ceiling lights need to go and where you might need extra sockets for lamps.

☐ If you are replacing the flooring then consider adding sockets into the floor – that way you can have a lamp on a table behind the sofa even if the sofa is in the middle of the room rather than having to trail a lead across from the wall.

☐ You need to layer the lights in a room. This means a mix of ceiling, floor, task and table lamps will all be needed so they can come on at different times and create different atmospheres depending on what is going on.

☐ Put ceiling lights on different circuits so you can decide if you want bright light in one part of the room and low light in another. This is good for a kitchen-diner where you might want the cooking area in shadow and atmospheric lighting in the dining area while you eat, whereas in the living room you might need to make it dark to watch a film as well as a light spot for reading.

☐ If you are adding lights to a room then consider dimmers essential.

☐ Good lighting will hide a multitude of furniture sins – or cheap furniture. It's the same as the old trope that candlelight is flattering to the skin.

☐ Think about lighting in the way you think about makeup. Use it on the walls to enhance a good feature – a painting or a collection of ornaments on a table. Use it to decorate and highlight a dark corner – or conversely leave it dark if it's just playing host to the vacuum cleaner.

☐ Just because a pendant light starts out in the middle of the room doesn't mean it has to stay there. Extend the flex and fix a cup hook to the ceiling and then you can hang it wherever it will be most useful in the room. This can be in a corner to save floor space if you don't have room for a table but want to illuminate the chair. Try swapping a single ceiling rose for a multi and then you can hang a light at either end of the sofa – another space saving trick. Or drop one low over the coffee table to highlight what's on there and provide a decorative focal point.

COOKING & DINING

72 WHAT IS THE BEST KITCHEN FLOORING?

As with many things it's a question of taste, and there are pros and cons for all. I have reclaimed floorboards and I like the slightly rustic feel which contrasts with the modernity of the units, but that makes it more complicated to install underfloor heating, and radiators take up precious wall space (see Q23 for advice on installing underfloor heating).

If you have underfloor heating then tiles or engineered wood can be a good idea (Q21). Watch out for the grout though. White grout discolours really fast and the smaller the tiles the more grout there will be. While we're on the subject I'm going to make a controversial statement – it's my book so I can – I really don't like large grey tiles. I know that there's a fashion for blending the inside and out but it just looks like a big slab of pavement. In the

UK where the light is often grey, adding a grey floor just exacerbates the issue. Why not think about a warm terracotta tile? Vintage looks great, but modern works too, then if you really want to match to the outside you can have bricks laid.

Or consider a pattern. Kitchens are all hard surfaces and straight lines, so adding some pattern on the floor can look wonderful. You don't have to go crazy with the colour scheme – black and white, or charcoal and ivory can work really well if you don't want the busyness of an encaustic pattern.

Cement floors are also fashionable, although they will be more expensive than you think, as they need polishing. Resin is another option. Both of these are seamless, thereby avoiding the issue of dirty grout, and also work well with underfloor heating.

73 WHAT IS THE BEST
WORK SURFACE?

Installing a new kitchen presents a thousand and one options and can seem like the most decisions you have ever had to make on anything at any time, so you probably only want to do it once – which means you want to get the work surfaces right.

The first point is that you don't have to have the same work surface throughout. These days it's perfectly acceptable to have one material on the island and one by the sink, for example. If you have been paying attention to the big six questions, by now you will have a fairly clear idea of what you want to be doing in this room and this will inform your choice.

The most practical material, and the one you find in restaurant kitchens, is stainless steel. It won't scorch, warp or stain, and you can have the kitchen sink made from one seamless piece, which is both hygienic and prevents water damage. That said, not everyone likes that industrial look. One solution is to have stainless steel around the sink and the hob, and something more tactile and warmer on the island or breakfast bar.

Wood, which is the cheapest option, is very pleasant to sit at and warm to touch, but it is prone to black mould around the sink and black burn marks by the cooker.

Marble is beautiful but, as a natural material, it is porous. It can stain – lemon juice, turmeric and splashing tomato sauce will do untold damage if you don't seal it regularly. And are you going to? The same can happen with granite. Also, if you drop a glass on a stone work surface it won't bounce. But if you like the look of stone then consider the composites. Companies like Caesarstone and Silestone make work surfaces from pulverized quartz, which is then mixed with resin. It looks like the real thing but it's much less temperamental. They can even mend it for you if you drop a heavy pan and it chips.

Polished concrete, which comes in and out of fashion, is much more expensive than you might imagine and it's porous, so it will stain. It's also (stating the obvious) heavy, which means you may not be able to add it to budget-friendly carcasses as they may need reinforcing to take the weight, which will of course, add to the cost.

Corian, which is moulded in a single piece and will have no visible joins, is very expensive and can feel a bit plasticky for all that money.

Laminate is the cheapest. It's much, much better than it was in the 1970s and easy to install, although any joins will be very visible.

And yes, we've all been on holiday and lusted after the rustic tiled work surfaces in the holiday cottage. Looks great when new, but when used daily the grout will stain and it's not the most hygienic. If you don't actually cook much then go for it. After all, at that point it's just a style statement.

74 HOW MUCH SPACE DO I NEED FOR AN ISLAND OR PENINSULA?

One of the most common questions I'm asked about kitchens is whether you have enough space for an island.

When we were planning our kitchen and doing the extension, we spent a happy evening in the half-built room laying planks on the earth floor and moving around them while drinking Aperol Spritzes. Basically, an island can be any size you want but it does need to have a minimum of 1m (3ft) around the sides to give you room to move around it. If you can have that, you can have an island.

Less than that and it becomes too tight to manoeuvre comfortably – you need to imagine yourself getting through with a handful of plates from the table, or a basket of laundry etc. In my house we arrived at 110cm (43in), which is perfectly comfortable for my 5ft 6in. We do have 90cm (35½in) at one end, and it's a little tight, but OK. The way to work out the optimum distance is to see if you can pivot between island and wall units without taking a step. So, in my kitchen, it was a case of can I fill a pan with water and

pivot to the hob with it? Taking a small step is no good – it won't happen naturally and you're more likely to trip. That measurement allows us to have two people behind the counter and elbow a fridge-lurking teenager out of the way.

How big should it be? Well, again that depends on the available space. Since a standard UK cupboard unit is 60cm (23½in) deep, that's the narrowest you will go. We have added a second row of cupboards – technically wall cupboards – that are 30cm (12in) deep behind to make it 90cm (35½in) – and covered the island with a 120cm (47¼in) work surface that overhangs down one side to make a bar with stools. You can go wider, of course, but you will need a big room and it might look like there is a cruise ship sailing down the middle of your kitchen.

If, for size reasons, you can't make a freestanding island work, attaching it to the wall at one end creates a peninsula that is just as practical and can work as a really good dividing area between kitchen and dining spaces.

75 WHAT **SHAPE** SHOULD MY **DINING TABLE** BE?

Most of us won't have enough space to have much choice when it comes to the size and shape of our dining table, but if there is any room for manoeuvre it's worth thinking about. A rectangular table for six or eight will mean several different conversations going on at once. A round table will keep the conversation together more. King Arthur knew what he was doing when he invited his knights over for dinner.

And we need to talk about size. A table, of any shape, needs at least 1m (3ft), between it and the walls for chairs to pull out, and for people to be able to walk around. If you have a rectangular room and more than two people to feed, you will probably need a rectangular table. But round tables are not only better for conversation – everyone can reach the potatoes. If there are four people then it needs to be about 1m (3ft) in diameter – less is doable but tight. If you can't fit that, think about an extending table.

Now you also need to consider the legs. Where will they be in relation to where the chairs will go? And then think about how it might look with, as Eero Saarinen put it, 'a slum of legs' – which led directly to his design classic Tulip table and chairs with their tidy single pedestal supports. For years we had an old art school table in the kitchen. With a chunky square leg at each corner it really dominated the space as well as being slightly too high for modern day chairs, so look out for that when buying vintage – 76cm (30in) is about the average height for a table, with 45cm (18in) for a chair. We replaced it with a table that was wider and longer with a much thicker top, but because it had two metal trestle-style legs tucked underneath, it was less dominant in the room. Everyone who came round asked if we had bought a smaller table. It was an optical illusion.

Once you have chosen the table, the chairs need to follow. If you're worried about budget (who isn't?) I would suggest spending more on the chairs, which need to be comfortable, than what is essentially a slab of wood to rest the plates on. If space is tight, benches are good, and while they aren't as comfortable for long, lazy dinner parties, you can tuck them away under the table when not in use.

Folding chairs are handy for extra seating, and can be tucked away when not needed. Otherwise, buy chairs for the people who will be sitting on them and eating there for 325 days of the year. If you want eight chairs for Christmas but there are two of you and two high chairs for the rest of the year, maybe a bench is the answer after all.

Based on @hygge_for_home

76 WHAT ABOUT OPEN SHELVES VERSUS CUPBOARDS?

This one is going to come down to personal preference. Open shelves are currently the fashionable choice as there is a move towards creating kitchens that don't look like kitchens – ie that aren't all fitted cupboards and often aren't fitted at all. The idea is that you are furnishing a room in which you cook and wash up rather than one that is fitted out with sleek, ergonomic, high-tech gear.

Open shelves fit with that look but you need to be able to create enough hidden storage to put the ugly appliances or things that won't look so pretty on the shelves. On a practical note, open shelves will get dusty. Now, I keep things I use every day on mine so for the most part it's not too bad, but

there are definitely mugs at the back and champagne glasses on the top shelf that aren't used all that often and will need a rinse before they can be pressed into service. In addition, I wouldn't have open shelves next to, or either side of, the hob as they, and their contents, will be splashed with cooking fat and grease and covered in steamy condensation. In my kitchen the hob is on an island and the shelves are on the wall about 1.6m (5¼ft) away, so cooking fumes aren't an issue.

Let's compare that with cupboards. One of the issues I have with wall cupboards is that they tend to be fitted so low that the less accessible space at the back of the work surface inevitably becomes a store for freestanding stuff like kettles and coffee pots, thus narrowing the available workspace (the area in front of the wall cupboards) from the UK standard depth of 60cm (23½in) to nearer 30cm (12in). So, if you do want wall cupboards, try and set up a system that leaves at least part of this space clear. If you are starting from scratch and have the space then consider bringing the base cupboards forward by about 30cm (12in).

But cupboards can create a tidier and more minimal look with everything out of sight, and if you live in an open-plan space, that can be more desirable. If you do have cupboards then you must make sure they go all the way up to the ceiling, which will not only make the ceiling look higher, but also prevent you putting stuff on the top that will just sit there and collect dust. Just continue the cupboard all the way up to the top and then you can still store the things you don't need but they will be behind a door and dust-free.

If you're buying standard cupboards that don't reach that far, make friends with a carpenter (see Q52). You can have new doors made that reach to the top – creating a slightly false front – or you could have a row of small cabinets made along the tops to fill the gap.

So now you know the pros and cons, it's up to you.

77 HOW MUCH STORAGE DO I NEED?

More than you think. Although it is a truth not really acknowledged that there is no such thing as a house that is too small, just a person with too much stuff. It's not so much 'how much storage do I need?' but 'do I need to store it?'

When I designed the open shelves in my kitchen I made drawings of everything I wanted to put on them and how much space I was going to allow. Then the extra stuff went into cupboards and from there to the charity shop.

You need to think realistically about how much of everything you actually need. Do you need to keep everything you have? Some decluttering experts suggest that no one really needs more than six mugs. I've definitely got about 20. And what about glasses? I've got small tumblers, large ones, vintage ones and coloured ones. I need a clear-out. All of this is fine if you have the space but if you don't then you need to get rid.

When it comes to saucepans I'm very disciplined – we were given a set of three and a metal steamer as a wedding present 20 years ago and that seems to be enough. I once wanted a cupboard just for Tupperware and while I managed to create that it wasn't long before I realized it was basically just a repository for 27 mismatched lids and random bases – none of which fit together. So that went. Now, it's full of light bulbs – none of which seem to fit any actual light I own – as well as two rarely deployed blenders, a juicer, and two electronic mashers. I feel a clear-out coming on…

78 WHERE YOU SHOULD SPEND MONEY IN THE KITCHEN?

Generally speaking I advise against cheap taps and appliances – when it comes to things with working parts you should always buy the best you can afford. I once bought a cheap tap with a pull-out hose because it looked nice, but the hose broke and the company had gone bust – or weren't responding to their customer service emails. I had to buy a new tap. 'Buy cheap, buy twice', as the saying goes.

As with fashion, buying 'labels' can help with resale, so if budget allows, buy the best and include it in the sale price or take it with you when you move. We have always bought cheap washing machines and, yes, I know it's a very controversial habit to keep the washing machine in the kitchen, but the point is that in the time my friend, who was given a Miele as a wedding present nearly 20 years ago, has had hers, we have had four machines and paid for countless repairs. 'Shoulda bought Miele' has been the refrain in this house many a time.

Talking of appliances and gadgets, let's take a moment to talk about cooker hoods. They are phenomenally expensive and most people think they don't work very well. Don't buy the fancy ones that look like chandeliers – they don't actually look like chandeliers, or work any better than the others. On the whole, extractor fans work better if they are ducted to the outside rather than just recirculating the air in the room, but they aren't always an option. A hood over an island is even more expensive and the kicker is that for it to work properly it will need to be quite low over the hob, which means it will probably be in the sightline of the person cooking, who wanted an island hob so they could chat to people at the same time.

However, there is another way. You don't have to have a cooker hood at all, as long as you have a good extractor fan on the wall. Most hoods will extract at the rate of 15L per minute. But you can fit a wall fan anywhere in the kitchen as long as it extracts at 30L per minute and is ducted to the outside – which is much easier as it's already on the wall and you don't have to run pipework along the kitchen ceiling and outside. It will be cheaper and more discreet than an overhead fan but I'm not going to promise the smoke alarm won't go off when you fry a steak. Make sure Building Control will pass it as acceptable, though.

79 WHERE CAN I SAVE MONEY ON MY KITCHEN?

The path of budget carcasses that are pimped with fancy handles and even door fronts is well trodden. Head to the giant Swedish superstore on the outskirts of town and buy the basics

from there (other budget kitchen companies do exist but they don't all allow you to buy only the parts you want). Then you can acquire new doors. Lots of companies make them to fit these days but it isn't necessarily going to be the cheapest. That would be to buy a sheet of MDF and have doors cut to fit by your friendly carpenter. If you want to make them more interesting, you can rout out a few straight lines to add personality. Cutting out a finger hole instead of paying for handles will create a minimal look that saves money too.

Plain tiles make the most affordable splashbacks, although if you're worried about grout getting stained then a large piece of glass will solve that and also act as a place to write shopping lists and reminders. Or you can use coloured grout (see Q93). Cooker hoods are often insanely expensive and routinely don't work well anyway (see Q78 for an alternative). See Q73 for advice on different types of work surface, from frugal wood to posh polished concrete.

80 WHAT ABOUT **GADGETS** IN THE **KITCHEN?**

Now, I'm not suggesting the kitchen should be full of expensive fancy gadgets but if that is going to make you happier to be in there or help you with the boring jobs then I'm all for it. I also think that every kitchen should include one gadget that lessens the load. For me it was a boiling water tap, not least because it removed the need for a kettle on the work surface and kept it looking clearer and clutter-free. It also means instant cups of coffee (not instant coffee, you understand, just instantly ready). You may prefer a wine fridge or a steam oven.

If a dishwasher is your dream but you live alone and feel it's not justified then look for the ones that come with two drawers that operate independently of each other. Personally, I don't like those fridges that deliver cold water or ice cubes, as you have to plumb them in and that's another job. A fridge with a small door inset into the larger one so that you can just reach in and grab the milk, however, is a good idea.

And while we're on the subject, do you need that big fridge? In my experience the size of the fridge is directly proportional to the number of half-finished jars of sauce and pickles that live on the top shelf. We had an under counter fridge for a family of four for six years. We planned our menus and wasted very little food. Christmas was tricky, yes, but you can't buy furniture just for the one or two days of the year when it might really be needed, as I said earlier about chairs (see Q75).

When it comes to the oven, it's about what suits you best. A range cooker looks fancy and costs more than a standard built-in oven. And might you actually quite like an eye-level oven that saves bending down? It's also out of the way of small children, which isn't something that's an issue for long, but the bending down might be.

So if you are redoing the kitchen, and there is anything left in the budget, then think about a treat.

81 WHAT IF MY **KITCHEN** GOES OUT OF **FASHION?**

This is basically a question about colour, and one I am asked regularly. The kitchen is one of the biggest investments you will make in your home and everyone is so terrified of getting it wrong that they end up making really safe choices that don't necessarily reflect their taste and personality and, it must be said, don't make them happy.

Years ago, I wrote a feature for a newspaper about the new fashion for glass work surfaces. They could be made in every colour of the rainbow, said the manufacturer – orange, lime, raspberry... 'And what do people choose most often?' I asked. 'White,' came the sad reply.

If you are doing up a kitchen with a view to selling, or know that you are in a five-year house as opposed to a forever home, then sensible (read white) might be the way to go. You can always paint the walls instead. But let's assume that's not the case. If you have wooden cupboard fronts, then you can of course paint them as often as you change your mind. I feel strongly that your kitchen, in which you probably spend a lot of time, should be filled with the colours that make you happiest. And you know what they are. You probably wear them. Or have a picture hanging in the living room that

is full of them. I would advise that you don't go for the brightest or strongest one because that might be a little overwhelming, and it's true you might get bored with it more quickly than you would with a gentler version.

Alternatively, there is no earthly reason why the base cupboards have to match the wall cabinets. So go bold on the bottom half and then match the wall units to the walls to create a more open sense of space.

Ultimately, this is about knowing yourself and your style and hopefully, by this stage of the book, you are finding that out. I once had a client who wanted advice on the colour of her kitchen. At the time everyone was painting everything grey and she thought she would, too. But I could sense a reluctance to commit. We spoke about the other rooms in the house and the clothes she liked to wear. Eventually I suggested navy. 'That's exactly the colour I want, but I didn't realize until we started talking,' she said. The grey testers were binned. The lower cupboards were painted navy blue and since it was an open-plan room, the sofa, which too was navy, worked perfectly. So the two spaces were tied together without them being too matching. Sometimes you just have to trust your instincts.

HOW TO PLAN A KITCHEN: A CHECKLIST

☐ Work out what is wrong with the current layout so you know what to put right.

☐ Know your budget – is this about changing cupboards, handles, work surfaces etc or a more fundamental rip out and start again?

☐ Visualize how you use the space – carrying plates from table to dishwasher, putting the plates away, making coffee and toast etc.

☐ Use the Who, What, When, Where, Why and How method from the introduction to get the details right.

☐ Consider what sort of cook you are, as this (and your budget) will inform the work surface. Natural stone is porous and will stain, wood is cheaper but hates water and hot pans.

☐ Classic colours are always good in kitchens as you don't want to be too trend led, but if you love a colour then use it. Alternatively, bring in some splashes of colour in the accessories, which you can easily change.

☐ Every kitchen should have one treat in it if at all possible – mine is a boiling hot water tap, yours might be a steam oven or a wine fridge.

☐ Don't forget the lighting – use task lights in the work area, but have them on dimmer switches and different circuits so you can light parts of the room instead of the whole. Consider wall and table lamps as well for more ambient lighting.

☐ The kitchen is, ultimately, another room in your house. Make sure it still reflects you and your taste. If the rest of your house isn't modern, don't let a kitchen installer talk you into a sleek contemporary look if that just isn't you.

☐ Consider having different work surfaces in different areas – wooden for the bar and composite by the sink. Do the same with the floor – tiles in the food prep area and floorboards in the eating area. It's not about one size fits all, it's about picking the size that fits you.

☐ When space around the dining table is tight, benches are a great seating solution. If you're worried they will look uncomfortable you can always dress them with a sheepskin (very Noma!). And if you're really worried they will be uncomfortable, add a foam seat cushion covered in a fabric of your choice.

LOUNGING & WORKING

82
WHAT IF I
DON'T HAVE ROOM
FOR AN OFFICE?

You will have to carve out a little spot from another part of your home to work at.

If that needs to be the kitchen table then that's fine, but find somewhere to store papers and printers etc. The paperless office is much closer – you can now scan a lot of documents and store them in the cloud, but there are still times when things need to be printed and kept. I worked at the kitchen table for many years and kept a plastic box on wheels with a lid under the table for all the 'officey' stuff that I needed on a daily basis.

I have written about creating an office in a cupboard (see Q83), but sometimes it's just about finding a handy corner to work in. Perhaps you can buy a desk that is a table with a drawer so you can slide the notebook and laptop into it at the end of the day and leave it clear overnight. If it's a corner of the bedroom then see if you can fit in a screen so that you can, as it were, put it away and hide it from view in the evening.

In a spare room, it's all about making clever furniture choices. First of all, buy a sofa bed. This is a good idea anyway, as it will free up more space in the room and who doesn't want that? I am constantly astounded by how many people don't think of that. Also, working in a room with a bed in it is an inherently bad idea.

Next up – can you work from a table that can double up as a dressing table? Keep the mirror and vanity items in a drawer and then whip them out when guests arrive and put the desk stuff in the drawer. Yes, this is harder if you have a large desktop computer, in which case you will just have to live with that. Consider putting Shaker pegs all around the walls too – these work well as decoration and you can also hang baskets with paper and stationery supplies in too. Plus they are perfect for guests who may only have a couple of things that need hanging, but they can also use them for a towel, a dressing gown and even a toiletry bag.

83

HOW TO CREATE AN OFFICE IN A CUPBOARD

Not all of us have the room for a dedicated office so we have to carve out an area in another room. The most important thing is to be able to shut it away at the end of the day. We all know that the blue light from the phone screen or the computer is bad for us when we sleep – which is why it's not great to have the office in the bedroom. But, sometimes, needs must. In that case think about putting your desk in the wardrobe.

In the first flat I rented in London with my husband (then boyfriend) we did exactly that. There was one living room that had the sofa and the dining table, and a large bedroom that had a mattress on the floor (we would be together for five years before we owned a real bed) with a wall of fitted wardrobes. So, we stuck a small table in there with a chair and bunged the computer on top. I'm not sure it even had a light in it, but this was in 1995 so the eerie green glow from the screen worked well enough. In more recent times, we would have had a laptop and probably worked from the sofa – as I am doing now.

That's the basic idea, but you can create something much more specific and, incidentally, this is also a good idea for a child or teenager's bedroom if they need a place to do homework but also want to shut it away at night.

Ideally you would build your desk cupboard into an alcove. Put a shelf at desk height (standard height is about 73cm/28¾in – for more standard measurements, refer to the checklist on page 102) with a stool that slides under, or a chair if you have enough space. Put shelves above, spaced office file height apart. Make sure there are sockets for a desk lamp (consider a clamp light for a shelf), the printer (which can sit under the desk) and all the relevant bits that need charging. You can also insist the phone goes in there overnight. Add double doors – these will take up less space when open and, as is often the case if the alcove is next to a window, will block less light when open. You can do this in a large kitchen too if you can afford to surrender food storage space, or anywhere a cupboard can fit.

As a final touch, think about painting the inside a colour that makes you happy so that when you open the door you feel pleased to be seeing that space and not full of doom and dread at the

thought of the work ahead. You can even add a fitted desk on a landing, although it's probably better to get your carpenter to design something bespoke, as you can have it made to fit exactly, without sacrificing precious space. (See Q52 on why you need to make friends with a carpenter.)

If you have filled your alcoves – or a wall – with bookshelves, then consider removing one shelf at desk height and use the same trick – this time install a single double-depth shelf to give yourself desk space. There's no chair storage with this but you can always keep a chair or stool to one side.

84

HOW CAN I MAKE MY OFFICE
INSPIRATIONAL?

We spend ages styling the mantelpiece or arranging the kitchen shelves, but our workspace often gets left behind. When you only have a small room or space to function as a home office, it's easy to get so caught up in the practicalities that you can overlook the importance of how inspirational the décor needs to be.

No one wants to sit in a space which feels draining and depressing, or to feel cross at the thought of having to be in there at all – even if there is a super-duper slidy drawer for the keyboard to slip in and out of and a state-of-the-art filing system. I have already written about the importance of getting the wall colour right (see Q83) so that it's a place that makes you feel happy and creative (green is good for that btw), but don't forget the other details.

A giant noticeboard isn't just for unpaid bills and reminders. Making a space on the wall for a board that you can rearrange as the mood suits you will turn it from being a purely functional space into one you use to transform your dreams into reality. So add things to keep you inspired; a picture of that fabulous holiday you've been working towards, a ticket stub from that gig or film you went to a few months ago when you had such a great evening. I always have large swatches of my current favourite paint colours stuck on mine. Why not use one of those apps to download and print a few pictures from your phone of fun times and pin them up alongside that page you tore out of that magazine just because you liked it? Some say that sticking up pictures of the things you want is a good way to manifest them into existence or, on a less woo-woo note, to spur you into working harder so you might be able to pay for them.

If you don't want a board – either cork tiles or magnetic – then what about a couple of floating shelves on which you can prop that magazine with the great cover as well as this month's edition that you still have to read, plus a couple of ornaments, some keepsakes, and a calendar. I use the shelves in my office as a sort of permanently shifting moodboard – a curated collection of my favourite things – that often provides much-needed Monday inspiration (more of which you'll find on the blog).

85 HOW DO I
CHOOSE A SOFA?

There are endless guides on buying sofas which seem to tell you nothing more than pick a style and a colour that you like and make sure it will fit through the door. Those are not irrelevant points, but they are the details. After a mattress (see Q51 and Q56), I think a sofa is the second most important purchase you will make and, given the expense, one that you will want to last for several years. So here are some things to bear in mind when choosing (I'll leave you to work out the colour and style yourselves).

First of all, the frame should be hardwood. Some sofa companies use part hardwood and part chipboard, which will deteriorate over time. This mix also allows them to claim that it's hardwood. Always ask before you buy. The frame should be both heavy and rigid. Check this by lifting it from the front. If it flexes, it's not strong enough.

If you're not sure if it will fit, then you need to measure the access points and be aware of landings and turns on stairs. Use masking tape to map out the space it takes up on the floor in the room you want to put it in and, if necessary, send a picture of the stairs to the manufacturer so they are forewarned. Some models come with removable arms and legs, and some companies will even modify a design by a few centimetres for you.

When it comes to style, bear in mind that narrow arms mean more sitting space. Tall legs mean you will see more of the floor, which makes the room look larger (see Q9). We will look at which fabric to choose later (Q86), but when it comes to cushions you should know that feathers will always need plumping and foam isn't as comfortable, so try and find a mix. Feathers wrapped in foam is a good solution as it's comfortable and won't need too much 'fumffing' (technical word).

SOFA SHAPES

This is about thinking back to those original big questions and deciding who is going to be using the room with the sofa in it, what will they be doing on that sofa, and how much space you have. A curved sofa can look wonderful and needn't take up a huge amount of space, but it's a conversation sofa not a box-set watching sofa. A modular sofa is great for stacking up all the children and watching a film but they (sofas not children) will take up a lot of room and might not work in a narrow Victorian terrace. You should also bear in mind that there will always be a fight over who gets the end bit where they can put their feet up. For everyone else it's the coffee table.

86 WHAT MATERIAL IS BEST FOR SOFAS AND CHAIRS?

Velvet has become massively popular in recent years, particularly for sofas and chairs. But there are two types, and one of them is tougher than the other. Man-made velvet has no nap, it can be stain-resistant and is much, much tougher than cotton velvet. This may have a nap that will brush the wrong way, hates stains and is generally more delicate. That said, velvet is generally tougher than linen, which can just rub away (especially if the sitters wear jeans regularly). I would recommend a man-made velvet over a linen any day. Yes, even with toddlers.

Talking of rub, you need to find out about the Martindale (Wyzenbeek in the US) rub test. This is an industry standard calculator which counts how many times a piece of fabric can be rubbed before it breaks down. A good industry standard is 35,000 for a domestic material but you will often see scores of 30,000 too. A tough man-made velvet can score 100,000, but more usual is around 65,000. Basically, the higher the better.

But the Martindale rub test is just that – rubs. It won't tell you anything about stains or fading. So, you also need to know that dark fabrics will fade faster than pale, and cotton and linen fade faster than velvet. Many fabrics now have inbuilt stain resistance and lots of companies are now working to improve fade resistant qualities as well.

Sadly, no one has yet developed anything that is pet resistant. For that you will need a water pistol.

87

WHAT ABOUT THE
COFFEE TABLE?

Like bedside tables (see Q99) these can be hard to get right. First, make sure it's sitting fully on the rug and that the rug is anchored by the furniture around it. We don't want coffee table boats marooned on rug islands.

Next up, you have to decide on the purpose of your table, and this may well be dictated by the size of your room. In most cases you need to allow 90cm (3ft) to walk comfortably past a piece of furniture, but I like to have my coffee table a leg length away from the sofa. This, of course, will vary from person to person. This also tells you that I like a coffee table that isn't fancy. Mine is a large old thing that I picked up from a junk shop. It can hold a couple of piles of glossy books, a vase of flowers and a pretty candle or two, the cheeseboard, a bottle of wine, the cat and my feet. If that sounds like your ideal table then you need to hit eBay. One option is to buy an old kitchen table and cut the legs off, which is how I strongly suspect mine came to be, albeit 200 years ago.

If you are a more genteel sort of character who wants the coffee table to hold a cocktail and a display of beautiful objets d'art, then consider glass or marble. If the room is small, then try to find one with thin legs, or a glass top, or one made from rattan or brass – something that will allow the light to flow through so that it doesn't look like there's a beached whale in the middle of the room. If you think you might need extra seating, then an upholstered ottoman style piece can work really well. Just make sure you have a large tray for drinks and meals.

And, of course, you don't have to have just a single coffee table. The nest has come back into fashion as a hugely practical piece. Traditionally this was kept to one end of the sofa with the extra tables being pulled out as required, but these days you can have all three in front of the sofa at differing heights and just move a single one closer to you when required. This can look particularly good with a set of two or three round tables, as their curves provide a good contrast to the likely rectangle of the sofa.

88 HOW CAN I HIDE THE TELEVISION AND WIRES?

One of the most commonly asked questions I ever hear. First of all, consider painting the wall behind the TV dark. That way it will disappear into the décor. But not everyone wants dark walls, so that won't work for all.

Another trick is to create a false section of wall, behind which you can conceal all the sockets and wires if you have a wall-mounted TV, or it stands on a shelf with a shelf below for the boxes, soundbar, modem, and all the other stuff. First of all, if you're going for the shelf option get the electrician to install a row of sockets on the wall. Then cut a piece of plywood that fits the gap between the two shelves –

leave a finger gap or hole on either side for easy removal. Also cut out a space at the bottom for the wires to come out and plug into the appliances. When the appliances are on the shelves they will hide that gap. Paint the plywood to match the wall and bingo, it's all neat and tidy.

Other options include concealing your kit within a classic sideboard or storage cupboard. You could also put it behind a sliding door so that you only reveal it when you want to watch. This works on a large flat wall rather than an alcove as the latter means there is nowhere to slide the panel to.

89 WHEN SHOULD THE TV BE OVER THE FIREPLACE?

Never. It's basically too high for you to see it comfortably. It's like being in the front row at the cinema. Not to mention that you will have to chase out the wall to hide the wires and then make good and paint them. That's a lot more work than plugging it in when it sits on a small table. To find the right height for the TV, you need to draw a horizontal line from your eyes when you are sitting comfortably on the sofa to the point on the wall directly opposite. It will be lower than you think. Put the middle of the TV at that point.

90 HOW DO I MIX STORAGE AND DISPLAY?

This is key for the living room as it's likely to be the room where you have things you want to have on show, such as ornaments and coffee table books. Personally, I think all books look good on shelves, but I know lots of you prefer to put the racy paperbacks out of sight and just have the fancy hardbacks on show. I take a perverse delight in the pain on my husband's face when I place my Jilly Coopers adjacent to his Philip Roths, or refuse to put my dictionaries out of sight.

Whether you opt for traditional cupboards on the bottom with open shelves above, or floor to ceiling shelves with doors on some of them, you need to decide what comes out and what stays hidden. As a general rule, board games, DVDs (although I appear to be the only person left who still has those) and old magazines can go away, while ornaments, books and photographs can stay out. It may be a taste thing, but I prefer a shelf of family photographs to a wall of them.

91 HOW **HIGH** DO I HANG PICTURES?

Many people hang them too high, so the general rule of thumb is that the middle of the picture should be at eye level. Use common sense if you're 5ft 1 and live with someone who is 6ft 5.

Also if it's a giant painting, you don't want it too close to the floor. As a guideline, professional art hangers will suggest that the midpoint should be about 148–152cm (57–60in) from the floor. That is a good starting point if you are stuck, but actually it will be much more effective if you simply pay attention to the furniture in the room and use that as your guide.

The key is to create a relationship between the thing you are hanging and the thing it is hanging over. So, if you have a low bench or a table in front of a wall and stick a small picture above it, it may be too far away for the two pieces to work together. Ignore the rules and bring it lower or off to one side. I have found that taking a picture with a mobile phone can be a really good way of seeing how it actually looks. For some reason a photograph of the setup can be easier to gauge than real life.

For example, if you are putting a picture above a sofa, then the bottom of it should be about 30cm (12in) above the back to stop people hitting their heads on it. You will find a checklist with tips on arranging a gallery wall on page 172, but if you are just hanging a couple of pictures then there are some other points to consider.

Try to avoid the top of the picture being level with the top of a door or window as this creates too many straight lines. If you are hanging a picture opposite or within sight of a door, make sure you not only view the final position from inside the room, but outside where it will be visible.

If the picture seems too small for the space you have chosen, then rather than hanging it in the middle, where it will disappear, make a choice to place it low or off to the side, so that it will draw attention to itself. If you have a small picture that is too small for anywhere on its own, then pair it with a larger one and hang it below and off centre, so there is a relationship between the two.

In general, you want to avoid hanging one picture per wall. Aim, for example, for one large one on one wall, a group of three or four on another, a blank wall and another grouping that has a different number of pictures that are different sizes to the first grouping. The best way to work it out is to either lay the pictures on the floor in the way you want them on the wall, so you can

Based on @shoopy.studio
and @margoinmargate

see how they work together, or to use Command strips.

Beloved by stylists on shoots, Command strips are essentially sticky pads that pull apart – one goes on the wall and one on the picture. You can remove the strips from the wall without doing any damage. They are brilliant for gallery walls where you may want to move things around, as well as rentals where you may not be allowed to put holes in the wall. Adjust accordingly and fix with either strips or good old-fashioned picture hooks.

If you want to hang pictures in a straight line as part of a group – the most difficult, but to my mind the most effective – you need to mark your top line on the wall. Hold the frame up against it but with the picture facing the wall. That way you can measure the distance from the hook to the top of the frame and the line you have drawn. This works when there is a single hook. If your pictures have string, and all the strings are different lengths, I would either choose another pattern or swap all the string for pieces that are the same length.

And a final word on gallery walls – they can also look really effective when they are arranged around a corner, perhaps starting in an alcove and bending around onto the next wall rather than just sitting completely within the recess.

HOW TO ARRANGE A GALLERY WALL: A CHECKLIST

From Lisa Dawson, award-winning blogger, whose gallery walls in her Yorkshire home are Insta-famous and whose blog on the subject is her most popular post.

LISA DAWSON
AWARD-WINNING BLOGGER

- ☐ Find the right spot. Your gallery wall will be a focal point, a work of art in itself. Find a clear space and work out how much room you have to play with.

- ☐ Look at areas of your home that you wouldn't traditionally consider for a gallery – a display on a small landing can really add impact and personalize the space.

- ☐ Be clever with framing. Don't blow the budget on a custom service unless it's totally necessary. DIY superstores have a huge selection of ready-made frames.

- ☐ Spend some time working out which are your favourites – you want your wall to sing to you, so only pick art that you are passionate about. If you love it, include it.

- ☐ Juxtapose. Mix typography with photography; charity shop finds with oil paintings; limited-edition prints with holiday memories. The contrast will make your display more interesting.

- ☐ Lay it out. Use a rug similar to the size of your wall space as a template. Add frames one by one, moving them around until they are the perfect fit.

- ☐ Space it out. The frames don't need to match, but you do need to be consistent when you are planning. If you are mixing frame colours, ensure they're evenly spaced so that you don't have one block of colour.

- ☐ Get hanging. Transfer your frames on to the wall as per the rug floor plan. Start in the bottom left-hand corner and work your way upwards and outwards.

- ☐ Use the right fixings. For lighter, Perspex frames you can use Command strips, but for glass frames, gold picture nails are usually sufficient. For larger, heavier prints, it's worth drilling a hole for security.

- ☐ Be brave. Have confidence in yourself and your choices when it comes to choosing your prints and tackling the task.

BATHING & SLEEPING

92 WHEN CAN I **GET RID** OF **THE BATH?**

Many estate agents will tell you this is a mistake as you might deter future buyers. But I say you have to decorate for the people who live in your house and how they live now and not for a fantasy purchaser who may or may not turn up in 10 years' time – and who could quite easily put the bath back in, as the chances are they will want to change the décor anyway.

My mother, who is nearly 80, decided about 15 years ago that she wanted a walk-in shower as she no longer wished to climb in and out of the bath. The plumber advised her against getting rid of it altogether and she listened to him.

So now my mother has a bath that has been used once in all that time (by my younger son), a small corner shower and even a corner loo. It is not a luxurious space and she doesn't love it. But she didn't do it for herself, she did it for some notional future sale. And yet there is still a strong chance that any future buyer will want to change it anyway, if only because they don't like the loo in the corner.

So, if you use your bath as a giant towel rail, and your children prefer to shower, then get rid of it. It's your home. Not the plumber's. And certainly not the estate agent's.

93

WHAT ABOUT **GROUT?**

There are various cleaning solutions for grout that can be found on the internet. Some of which I have tried, many of which I haven't. None that I tried worked.

Grout always gets dirty when it's on the floor. One way to avoid that is to use dark grout to begin with. It will still be dirty, but it won't show. If you have a wet room shower with a tiled floor, the problem will be soap and shampoo. Clear versions of these can minimize the problem but won't prevent it altogether. Mapei makes their grout in a range of different colours, so you could contrast your white tiles with a pink grout, or use a gold grout between teal tiles. Think of it as an extra decorative feature.

Another contender is epoxy (or resin) grout. It's expensive and hard to use, so your builder probably won't be happy, but it is almost entirely stain resistant and will last significantly longer than traditional grout. We put it in our shower and, after a lot of complaining, our builder worked out how to do it and now recommends it in every bathroom he does. That is when he's not recommending micro-cement, which is a solid finish that needs no grout at all. Problem solved.

94

HOW MUCH
BATHROOM
STORAGE DO I NEED?

More than you think. A lot more. First of all, you need to think about what you need to keep in there – towels and spare loo roll? Or can that go somewhere else. How many bottles of shampoo are there likely to be on the go at one time? Invest in a rack for the shower or over the bath and keep everything that's needed for those two activities there.

You will need a cupboard under the basin, or a drawer. If you have bought a vintage piece to mount the basin on, then make sure it's a chest of drawers or a cabinet rather than just a table. Remember you will lose some space for the pipework.

If you have a wall-mounted loo, there is often a shelf over it where the cistern has been boxed in. Take shelves up to the ceiling from there. Or, if you're more private, put a door on it. Sophie Robinson, TV presenter and interior stylist, told me of a couple she knew who covered an entire wall of their bathroom in mirrored cabinets from Ikea. Not only will this make the space look bigger, but at about 21cm (8¼in) deep that's not much space to lose for the sake of a lot of storage. Although unless you labelled the doors it might turn into a giant game of hunt the needle in the reflective haystack.

In short, when the floor is full you need to use the walls. Think about how much storage you need and double it. I promise you the extra cupboard won't be empty for long.

95

WHERE SHOULD I
SPEND MONEY
IN THE BATHROOM?

You need to spend money on the bits that need to work – by which I mean the taps and flushing mechanisms and drains etc. We bought cheap taps for our bathroom basins and very quickly there was a tiny drip from one of the taps, which is now horribly stained and rough from limescale. Likewise, the cheap basins had plastic parts on the pop-up waste systems, which have since disintegrated entirely, so we have had to buy rubber plugs from Amazon.

When we were installing the shower, our builder warned us against a plastic shower tray as, he said, it would become unglued and sort of ripple underfoot over time. We ignored him, as a steel and enamel alternative was expensive. He was right. We replaced the shower tray within three years. In short, all the working parts should be the best you can afford.

When it comes to the bath, you may find you have a lot less choice than you think – acrylic is the lightest material, which makes it better for older houses. Cast iron freestanding tubs are very heavy. Steel baths can be expensive, so this may be one of the areas you can save on. Spend the money on high-quality taps instead.

It's also worth spending money on the parts that come into contact with water – think about shower screens, shower heads and valves. In addition, if you buy good quality and something does go wrong (and it shouldn't) you are more likely to be able to get a spare part rather than having to buy the whole thing again.

You can save substantially when it comes to the tiles. Some can be incredibly expensive, so shop around. And, of course, if you can paint the room yourself you will save there as well. It goes without saying that keeping the layout the same will save money on plumbing.

96 WHERE CAN I SAVE SPACE IN THE BATHROOM?

Britain builds the smallest houses in Europe – the average new-build in the UK is 76 sq m. Compare that with 137 sq m in Denmark (and people wonder

why the Danes are consistently found to be the happiest people in the world). For some reason bathrooms have always been shoehorned into tiny spaces (along with kitchens, which historically were just for the servants). In fact, the only time you tend to see really good-size bathrooms is in period properties where a bedroom has been converted. This means that most of us are trying to fit as much as we possibly can into a very tight space and still hoping it will feel luxurious.

If you want to keep the bath, then choose one that has a thin rim around it. A standard bath is 1700mm (67in) long (see the checklist on page 102) but that's the outside measurement. A traditional bath has a wide rim around it, which means less space for you once you're in. But new technology has allowed for the creation of baths that are like Dr Who's Tardis – bigger on the inside – because they are very thin.

If you want a bath and a shower but the latter needs to be over the former, then try and find a bath that rises vertically at both ends inside. This will give you more standing room than if it has a sloping end. And if you are standing in the bath to shower then make sure the plug is in the middle so you don't keep standing on it. If you do have a bath with a shower over it, then it is better to spend slightly more on the bath and choose a resin or cast iron one. This is because an acrylic one will flex as you stand in it and, over time, it will drop away from the silicone joint, which is what is keeping the water out of the room below.

Yes, you can buy short baths, although they won't give you that spa feeling, as you are basically half sitting in them. Far better, I think, to get rid of the bath altogether and install a bigger shower. Clear glass panels and a flush fitting tray that sinks into the floor will also create the impression of more space, as the design will appear to float. Keep the flooring the same throughout too.

You always need more storage in a bathroom than you think. And when you've run out of floor, remember to use the walls. If you've installed a wall-mounted loo – which is not only more hygienic but also shows more floor which will make the room *look* bigger – this may have created a shelf sticking out from where the hidden cistern has been installed. Use this as a base to add shelves up to the ceiling and add a door to keep the streamlined look.

Can you dig a hole out of the wall above the basin to set a cupboard into? This means the mirror will be flush with the wall but you have hidden storage – it only needs to be as wide as a bottle of shampoo or mouthwash, after all.

Heated towel rails can be bulky, and if you are using them to hang the towels then you aren't heating the room. Consider instead installing a couple of underfloor heating panels in the wall and fixing some hooks above. This will create a much more streamlined look.

HOW MUCH SPACE DO I NEED FOR AN EN SUITE BATHROOM?

If you want an en suite bathroom it's definitely worth looking at the area as a whole to see if you can steal space from the bedroom next door to create a more luxurious bathroom and dressing area. A big bathroom will always feel more luxurious than a big bedroom (see Q3), but sometimes there is no space to steal and your bedroom is a little bigger than you need, so the question is: is there enough space for an en suite?

I asked Louise Ashdown, the head designer at West One Bathrooms, for her advice. She said that if you are thinking of taking a corner of your bedroom then you will need a minimum of 1600 x 1600mm (63 x 63in) to allow for a corner shower. Choose a quadrant shape to allow yourself a little more elbow room when you are standing outside drying. You will also need 800 x 800mm (31½ x 31½in) for the loo and a basin, although you can get triangle loos that sit in corners and you can always fit a small cloakroom basin if you don't tend to splash a lot of water about.

However, a long thin room tends to work best – perhaps you can partition off one end or one side of the room?

Ideally, that needs to be a minimum of 1000mm (40in) wide – 1200mm (47¼in) is optimal – and 2000mm (80in) long. Put the door in the middle – a sliding door is best as it won't steal space from either room (see Q50). As you go in, put the shower, 1000 x 800mm (40 x 31½in), at one end, a wall-mounted compact loo at the other and a shallow basin in the middle.

Don't forget that you will need drying space as you come out of the shower and also to be able to turn around in front of the loo; so aim for a minimum distance of 700mm (27½in) in front of the shower and the loo to ensure you don't bang knees or elbows. This is the smallest space possible. It's best to go wider, if you can, with 1200mm (47¼in) and a minimum length of 2200–2400mm (87–94½in).

Now you will need to consider any sloping ceilings – particularly if men are involved. I saw an en suite in a loft with a sloping ceiling where everyone had to pee sitting down, which wasn't ideal. It might sound obvious, but don't forget that if you have storage with doors or drawers then you will need space to open them. The space in the middle of the room – for standing, drying, getting at the storage – is just as important as the amount of space you have in the shower.

Don't forget to check how noisy the flush is as it might wake you up in the night. A word on this: loos generally like to be as close to the soil pipe as possible. You can move them away from the outside wall but it may mean lifting the floor to achieve the correct 'fall' on the pipes. You also don't want too many bends and there will need to

be enough space under the floorboards for any pipework to slope slightly towards the soil pipe. A macerating loo (think about the name so I don't have to spell it out) can pump waste much further but they can also be noisy when flushed so bear that in mind if there's a lot of midnight activity.

And remember to consider the view from the room next door – you don't want to be looking at the loo when you're lying in bed.

98 HOW MUCH SPACE DO I NEED FOR A **WALK-IN WARDROBE?**

Again, it's worth looking at the space as a whole if you are looking to create a walk-in wardrobe. For a walk-through wardrobe like mine, I was advised by a friend who had a similar arrangement in her New York home, that you need to be able to walk through the space with your hands sticking out like a penguin. That's the walking/dressing bit. Then you need to add the hanger space onto that – both sides if you are lucky, just one if not – that's another 60cm (23½in).

If you are creating a false wall to put the bed in front of, then your width will be dictated by the size of the bed (plus optional bedside tables) and the access from the sides, which can be as narrow as a doorway, but 90cm (35½in) is optimal to give you a roomy and comfortable space to move.

Build your wall up to the ceiling – you can store things on high shelves at the back. If you don't have too many long dresses then put two rails in to maximize the storage – the lower one for trousers or at the height of the longest skirt (remember trousers can be folded over hangers), and one above for shirts and tops. We have only one rail (mine was a sort of prototype) but have recently put a low set of drawers from Ikea underneath for underwear, socks and gym kit.

Now, we have open storage, but I did include narrow doors (with a dip at the top) at either end of the walk-in wardrobe. The reason for this was twofold – one it's next to a window so that gave me some privacy from the house on the other side of the street, and two it's perfect for draping those clothes that aren't ready for the washing machine but you don't want to hang back up.

We also installed sockets so we could have lamps on the shelves to see what we're doing on winter mornings and in the evenings, although you may prefer a couple of spotlights. As we live in a traditional Victorian terrace, there is a fireplace with alcoves on either side. We use those for my shoes and extra hanging space and have put a large mirror over the fireplace, while the mantelpiece serves as a dressing table. I have put my makeup on standing up for so many years that the last time I sat down to do it (in a fancy hotel) I stabbed myself in the eye with the mascara wand.

WHERE DO I FIND GOOD BEDSIDE TABLES?

Everyone seems to have trouble finding good bedside tables. They are mostly a bit naff, for some reason. But if you do want them think carefully about what you require.

In my experience, bedside cupboards tend to be filled with rubbish that you don't actually need, and you end up putting the stuff you do need – water,

books, hankies – on the floor next to the bed, thus defeating the object. So, consider if you just need a drawer for lip salve and small things rather than a whole cupboard.

Whatever you have needs to be large enough for a lamp, a phone and its charger, a book or three, and possibly also a glass of water. There's a lot going on there. And it has to look good as well. That's an increasingly tall order. I tend to look for small vintage cupboards and cabinets – school-locker style works well.

Or perhaps you can have a shelf fitted by the side of the bed. Or two? That will free up floor space and, as we have established elsewhere, the more floor you can see, the bigger your room looks. If you are really tight for space you can also hang bedside lights from the ceiling (see Q68 for more advice about rethinking a pendant light), which gives you more room on the table for that pile of books that you're never going to read.

In short, as ever, think about what you really need to keep near you – and why – before you buy. Sometimes a pair of small occasional tables works really well. And no, they don't need to match, either.

100

HOW TO CHOOSE THE
RIGHT MATTRESS

The average person spends over 20,000 hours in bed – up to a third of their life. Buying the right mattress is key and I write as someone who slept on a mattress on the floor until my mid-30s. If you're about to invest, below is some advice from Hypnos, which has held a Royal Warrant since 1929.

Chris Ward, marketing director of Hypnos, says you need at least 10 minutes to truly get a feel for a mattress. Take off thick coats and possibly shoes, and lie in your sleeping position. Try with your partner, and if you both like different things then ask for a dual tension mattress, or a model with a central zip that allows you to join two separate ones together.

Size-wise, we usually tend to go for the largest one that will fit. As a guideline, we wriggle and turn between 60 and 70 times a night. Ideally, you should be able to lie on your back with your hands behind your head and elbows out and not touch the person next to you.

Think too about what will happen to your old mattress when the new one turns up. Typically, it's landfill, where they can take over 10 years to decompose and a double mattress will occupy around 23 cubic feet of space. Ask your new mattress provider if they offer a service that involves the deconstruction of the old one to create materials for re-use in other industries.

"A good mattress should support your whole body, regulate your body temperature and feel supremely comfortable. A sustainably produced one is also a bonus.

Pocket-sprung mattresses are the most expensive, but that is because they are designed to minimize the pressure points on the body. Each spring moves individually to mould itself to you and align your spine, which then alleviates tension and increases blood circulation, allowing the muscles to relax and you to sleep well. The other great thing about a pocket-sprung mattress is that if you are a different weight from your partner, or one of you is restless and moves around a lot, the springs will move individually and you won't both be tossing and turning like ships in a stormy sea.

Natural fibres are breathable so you don't overheat, and can help regulate body temperature in a way that synthetic ones don't.

HYPNOS

101

WHAT **BEDDING** IS BEST?

Because if you've read this far you probably need a lie down. It's largely a question of taste, but linen and cotton both have their pros and cons. There are also different types of cotton and I'll admit I was nearly 50 before I knew the difference, so I thought I would explain here.

First up a word about cotton – it takes huge amounts of water to produce so it's not necessarily an environmentally friendly choice. Having said that, this is a sector that has been massively disrupted in recent years and there are an increasing number of companies producing organic cotton in fairtrade factories employing women and using recycled rain water, so look out for those.

Now then, you're basically looking at percale and sateen – the latter, it turns out, is not cheap satin in a fancy soap opera, but refers to the length of the fibres used to make it. I didn't know that and have spent years avoiding sateen bedding because I thought it was fake satin. Anyway, listen carefully because here comes the science bit.

Thread count – as you probably know – is the number of threads per square inch. The basic rule of thumb when it comes to thread count is the higher the better. Only, of course, it's slightly more complicated than that. I spoke to Will Coulton, co-founder of Rise & Fall, about this. His company, which gives £3 from every sale to Centrepoint, the youth homelessness charity, works with a factory in India that runs on power produced by its own wind turbines, re-uses and recycles 99 per cent of its water, uses plastic-free packaging, and also ensures that the largely female workforce (and their families) have access to free education. He explained that if you have short cotton fibres, the machines knot them together, which makes the fabric feel rougher. The key is to have extra-long fibres, thus avoiding the knots and making the sheet softer. But you can also manipulate the thread count by packing the fibres more closely together, thereby increasing the count. This means the sheet will be heavier and may be rougher as well.

Percale is a weave of one thread over, one under, while sateen is one over and four under. Percale sheets should be no higher than 400 thread count or they will be hot and heavy to sleep under. Sateen should be 600. Clear?

Egyptian cotton comes from the plant *Gossypium Barbadense* and is the most prized because it has the longest fibres, but it isn't always grown in Egypt. So, don't be confused if you see Egyptian cotton from India.

Basically, if you want soft and snuggly then look for sateen, but if the crisp hotel feel is what you're after then go for percale. Or you can change with the seasons.

When it comes to linen, the fibres are generally thicker and longer than cotton and are more durable for that reason. Linen is made from flaxseed, which is a renewable source, so it is regarded as the greener option. You will also find people raving about the increasing softness of linen sheets the longer you have them, but it can take many washes to achieve this effect. Linen is also good at wicking away sweat so it's good at keeping you warm in winter and cool in summer. The pre-washed linen sets you can now buy on the high street are still more expensive than cotton and you may feel they're not quite soft enough for your purposes.

HOW TO PLAN A BATHROOM: A CHECKLIST

☐ Use the Who, What, When, Where, Why, and How method before you do anything.

☐ Do you need a bath or will a big shower be more useful and more luxurious?

☐ A flush-fitting shower tray is a good future-proof option, as you don't have to step up to get in.

☐ Have you got enough storage? Whatever you planned, add more.

☐ Can you fit two basins or one long one so more people can use it at once?

☐ A wall-mounted loo will make the room look bigger and is easier to clean around. The same goes for basins.

☐ Lighting needs to be on a dimmer for bright mornings and relaxing evenings.

☐ Tiles and mirrors will add personality and warmth. Treat this like any other room in your home and make sure it reflects you and the people who live there.

TOP TIPS FOR

RENTERS

&

FIRST-TIME

BUYERS

TOP TIPS: A CHECKLIST

There are ideas that will work for those who don't pay a monthly mortgage throughout this book, but here are the top ten gathered together in one place. These will also work for first-time buyers who have spent all their money on the bank loan and can now barely afford to eat, much less rip out kitchens and convert lofts.

☐ One of the main issues about renting is the difficulty of redecorating or being able to make the space feel your own. Peel-off wallpapers can help. The US has been ahead of the UK on this but you can find some great designs on Etsy.

KEY QUESTIONS: 5, 6, 7, 9, 10, 11, 12, 28, 29, 83, 84, 91

☐ Tiling is another area that can be fraught with bad taste in rental accommodation. You can paint them if the landlord permits. But you can also find an increasing number of tile stickers, which may be preferable as they are less permanent.

KEY QUESTION: 25

☐ Flooring can be a real problem. If it's hideous and you can't change it then rugs are your friend, as you can take them with you. Alternatively buy a large piece of carpet and have the edges hemmed to cover as much of the room as you can. Make sure you check the door will still open over the top of the second carpet as it will make everything much higher. Living in a first-floor flat, whether rented or bought, can often mean restrictions on wooden flooring for noise reasons, too. If you can swap carpet for seagrass or sisal then rugs work better on top of that.

KEY QUESTIONS: 13, 14, 15, 19

☐ You probably can't do much about moving the lights around, so spend money on good-looking lamps. You might be able to ask your landlord if their electrician can change the wiring and add a dimmer switch.

KEY QUESTIONS: 27, 63, 64, 65

☐ If you hate the curtains, then take them down, store them carefully, and buy some new ones. All the high-street homeware stores sell affordable curtains. Think about hanging two pairs per window for a more luxurious feel. And you can always buy simple blackout blinds and dispense with curtains altogether.

KEY QUESTIONS: 42, 43, 44, 45, 46, 47

☐ It's always worth asking if you can decorate – even if you're only allowed to use white, at least it will be fresh and clean and better than magnolia. You can then use washi tape (or similar) to create decorations and patterns on the walls that will peel off.

KEY QUESTIONS: 24, 25

☐ Find cheap old furniture that isn't worth anything financially and upcycle it. While a complete reupholstery job may not be on the cards, you can hide a multitude of sins with a piece of good material and a staple gun.

KEY QUESTIONS: 60, 61

☐ If you're not allowed to make holes in the walls, buy Command strips – these come in various different strengths and will hold most pictures. If you read the instructions carefully they will come off without bringing the paint as well.

KEY QUESTION: 91

☐ If you are there for a bit longer then consider changing kitchen cupboard door handles for something you like more.

KEY QUESTION: 48

☐ It's never a mistake to invest in pieces of furniture and accessories that you can take to the next place!

KEY QUESTIONS: 51, 55, 56, 57, 58, 60, 61, 62, 75, 81, 86, 87, 88, 100, 101

RESOURCES
NOTES FOR NORTH AMERICAN HOME RENOVATORS

The questions asked and answered in this book have no regard for geographic boundaries. Smart design is smart design on both sides of the Atlantic. Dimensions and construction specifics may differ however.

Keep in mind that not all building codes are standard across the U.S. Codes and restrictions might vary not just from state to state but from town to town as well. Some areas may have extra restrictions depending on designated flood zones and historical preservation districts. Other neighborhoods may have covenants limiting building heights, materials used and even choice of paint color.

You'll need to your homework first. Whatever the size and scope of your project, it's always best to seek out professional input. YouTube videos cannot solve every problem. Work with experienced contractors and trades people from your area who are familiar with local building codes and regulations. It helps if your team has a good working relationship with the building inspector as well.

DO MATTRESS SIZES VARY BY COUNTRY?

They do. A king-size mattress in Canada is at least a foot wider than the British king version. When planning a bedroom re-do, remember to factor in how much space the mattress plus bed frame will take up.

Standard Mattress Sizes US and Canada
Twin 38" x 75"
Full (aka double) 53" x 75"
Queen 60" x 80"
King 75" x 80"

WHAT ARE STANDARD SIZES FOR OFF-THE-SHELF KITCHEN CABINETS?

You'll find a wide range of configurations when buying pre-fab cabinetry.

Base cabinets: The standard height of the base cabinet is 34.5" without the countertop, 36" with the countertop. The toekick at the bottom measures 4.5". Standard depth is 24". Widths range from 9" to 47": the most popular are 30" and 36" wide.

Upper cabinets: Standard heights are 30", 36" or 42". Standard depth is 12". Some go up to 24" deep to accommodate installation over a refrigerator or wall-mounted oven.

Many manufacturers offer custom sizes as well without too great an upcharge.

HOW BIG IS THE AVERAGE AMERICAN BATHTUB?

A standard wall-to-wall bathtub measures 60" long and 30" to 32" wide. But today's bathtubs come in a number of nonstandard shapes and sizes from cozy corner tubs to small alcove tubs to oversized, free-standing oval tubs.

WHERE CAN I FIND GREENER PAINTS AND INFORMATION ON LEAD PAINT IN AMERICAN HOMES?

The EPA (Environmental Protection Agency) offers guidelines with links to paint resources on their webpage "Identifying Greener Paints and Coatings":
www.epa.gov/greenerproducts/identifying-greener-paints-and-coatings

Remodeling an American home built before 1978 may create lead-based paint dust. You should consider testing painted surfaces for lead before launching into a large-scale project. Home lead testing kits are available. Check the recommendations regarding lead paint found on the EPA's webpage:

www.epa.gov/lead/questions-and-answers-homeowners-and-renters-about-understanding-lead-inspections-risk

MUST I HIRE A LICENSED ELECTRICIAN FOR ALL ELECTRICAL WORK?

You don't need to apply for a permit to change a light bulb or to swap out a light fixture, but performing your own electrical work on more complex tasks brings with it a number of risks. Even if your local building codes do not require electrical work be done by a licensed professional, it's likely that any work to be done by an unlicensed worker will still have to be checked by the building inspector. Avoid the hassle and hire a professional at the outset.

The National Electrical Code (NEC) specifies acceptable wiring methods and materials for most states in the U.S. It requires that all outlet receptacles in a bathroom, kitchen and garage be GFCI-protected (ground-fault circuit interrupter), for instance. The NEC publishes revisions to its Code every three years. The Canadian Electric Code (CEC) governs standards in Canada.

WHAT IS THE DIFFERENCE BETWEEN AN IP RATING AND A NEMA RATING?

IP ratings (Ingress Protection) are an international standard that gauge the level of protection against dirt and moisture for electrical enclosures. Americans will see this rating on mobile phones, tablet computers and other hand-held devices. In the USA, the National Electrical Manufacturers Association defines NEMA enclosure types. Ratings between IP and NEMA ratings are not directly equivalent: NEMA ratings also require additional product features (such as functionality under icing conditions, enclosures for hazardous areas, knock-outs for cable connections and others) not addressed by IP ratings.

WHAT DO I NEED TO KNOW ABOUT INSTALLING A WOOD-BURNING STOVE IN THE U.S.?

Regulations for wood-burning heaters are stricter in Canada and the U.S. than in Britain.

Before you make a wood-burning stove the focal point of your renovated living area, have a licensed chimney cleaner inspect your chimney and chimney lining. (Some homes built before 1900 have unlined chimneys.) The chimney should extend at least 3 feet above the roof surface it penetrates. Chimney work can be expensive and you'll need to factor the cost into your budget.

And then there's the stove. No matter how charming your great-great-grandmother's Franklin stove is, haul it off to the scrap metal recycler. It's a polluter and possibly dangerous. When buying a new stove, check for the EPA-certification on the back of the stove. The Wood Heat Organization (woodheat.org) can answer all, or certainly most, of your questions about the responsible use of wood energy in your home. The EPA's webpage is helpful as well:

www.epa.gov/residential-wood-heaters

For wood-fueled heating in Canada, check out:
www.ccme.ca/files/Resources/air/wood_burning/pn_1479_wood_burning_code_eng.pdf

INDEX

alcoves 158–9, 169
antiques 113, 116, 119, 120
artwork 42, 113
Ashdown, Louise 181
atmosphere 37, 127

bartering 119
bathrooms 15, 25, 29, 173–82, 190
 decorating 67, 87, 178
 en suite 32, 100, 181–2
 hotel 34
 lighting 128, 129, 134
 space-saving ideas for 179–80
 standard measurements 102
 storage 51, 177, 180
 where to spend/save 178
baths 102, 175, 178–80, 194
bedding 188–9
bedrooms 120, 183–9
 allocation 32
 children's 61–2
 decorating 82, 83
 storage 51
beds 51, 111
 see also mattresses
bedside tables 186
bell curves 9–10
bespoke furniture 116, 118
blinds 92–3, 95, 97, 98
broken-plan living 46–7
budgeting 21, 24–5, 154
builders 21, 25, 36
building materials 21

building regulations 40

carpenters 106, 147
carpets 53–5, 61, 102, 120
ceilings 17, 24, 41, 43, 67, 81–2, 84, 120
cement flooring 139
CFL (compact fluorescent lamp) 123–4, 125
chairs 105
 antique 113
 comfy 41, 44, 46–7, 110, 115, 118, 120, 162
 dining 70, 112, 143, 154
 folding 45
 office 45, 159
 vintage 118
chandeliers 128
chests of drawers 118
children 46, 61–2
chimneys 109, 193
clothing 75, 115
coffee tables 41–2
cohesive looks 7
colour blocking 71
colour schemes 17, 29
 agreeing on 39
 for children's rooms 61, 62
 cohesive 70
 and the illusion of space 41
 inspiration for 34
 for kitchens 153
 and mixing colours 71
 and mood boards 36
 for narrow spaces 43
 and patterns 71

 picking the right colour 75
 starting out 29, 30
 using white 74
Command strips 169, 193
compact fluorescent lamp (CFL) 123–5
composites 140
compromise 25, 38–9
concrete, polished 140
Conservation Areas 31
contingency funds 21, 25
cooker hoods 149–50, 151
Corian 140
cotton 188–9
Coulton, Will 188
cupboards 42, 51–2
 all the way to the ceiling 51, 147
 bathroom 177
 bedroom 186
 kitchen 102, 146–7, 151, 193, 194
 living room 167
 offices in 157, 158–9
 see also wardrobes
Curphey, Philippa 113, 119
curtain linings 94
curtains 42, 94–5, 97, 98, 193
cushions 71

dado rails 84, 85, 96
damp 65
Dawson, Lisa 172
decluttering 51, 148
decorating see painting and

Index

decorating
desks 61, 158
Diffusion of Innovation
    Theory 9–10
dimmer switches 134, 136
discounts 18–19
dishwashers 152
door handles 99, 193
doors 89–102
    decorating 41, 68, 80, 120
    standard measurements
        102
    styles 68, 100–1
downlights 134
due diligence 40
Dulux 38, 66, 71
Duran, Kimberly 9–10
dust 51, 53, 146

'early adopters' 9, 10
'early majority' 9, 10
eco-paints 77
eggshell 66–7
electricians 17, 195
empty space 42
emulsion 66, 67, 76
en suites 32, 100, 181–2
engineered wood 57, 139

Farrow & Ball 67, 71, 78
feature walls 83–4
'feel of a room' 37
feng shui 51
fireplaces 24, 167, 193
first-time buyers 191–3
floor plans 31
floorboards 24, 120, 139
flooring 53–60, 270
    carpets 53–5, 61, 102, 120
    kitchens 139, 154

painted 67
renters 192
sockets in 136
see also rugs
form 14
framing 172
fridges 152
function 14
furniture 105, 110–20
    cheap 110
    children's 61
    expensive 110
    and lighting 134, 136
    mixing periods 114–15
    for multi-functional
        rooms 45, 157
    for narrow rooms 43–4
    for offices 157
    painting 116
    and picture hanging 168
    for renters 193
    for small spaces 41–2
    taking stock of your 29–30
    for TVs 164

glasses 148
gloss paint 66–7
granite 140
grout 67, 139, 141, 151, 176
    epoxy 176

Hall, Bianca 71, 85–6
halls 25, 66
halogen lights 123, 125
hinges 99
hotels 34
Hypnos 187

ideas, communicating your
    36

Ikea 19, 49, 102, 111, 116,
    177, 183
illusions 41, 43
Ingress Protection (IP) 128–
    9, 195
inside and out, blending 139
inspiration 34, 160
Instagram 9, 34
interior designers 9
investment buys 113

James, Tania 69

kitchen appliances 16, 149–
    52, 154
kitchen islands 48, 140,
    142, 149–50
kitchens 14, 15, 16, 20,
    137–54
    designer 105
    feel of 37
    flooring 139, 154
    lighting 134, 136, 154
    open-plan 46, 47, 48
    positioning 32, 33
    small 42
    storage 51, 102, 146–8,
        151, 193–4
    trends 153
    where to save 151
    where to spend 149–50
    work surfaces 140–1, 154
Knox, Karen 21, 24–5

'laggards' 9–10
laminate floors 53, 57
laminate work surfaces 140
lamps 19, 45, 126, 127, 134,
    136
landings 52, 66, 172

'late majority' 9
le Comte, Mary 71
light emitting diodes (LEDs) 124, 125
light fittings 123
light switches 25, 135
lighting 17, 25, 120, 121–36
   and atmosphere 127
   bathroom 128, 129, 134
   as divider 48
   kitchen 134, 136, 154
   living room 134
   natural 75, 78, 91
   pendants 132–3, 136, 186
   and renters 192
   requirements 126
   for walk-in wardrobes 183
   wall lights 126, 128, 129
linen 188, 189
lino 56
listed buildings 31
living rooms 15–16, 30, 37, 134, 161–9
Lloyd Wright, Frank 46
lumen 123–5

marble 140
Martindale rub test 162
mattresses 102, 105, 111, 187, 194
MDF (medium density fibreboard) 106, 116, 151
micro-cement 176
mirrors 42
moodboards 36, 37, 39
multifunctional spaces 45, 157

narrow rooms 43–4, 83
National Electrical Manufacturers Association (NEMA) 193

net curtains 98
new builds, adding character to 120
noticeboards 160

offices 32, 45, 155–60
open-plan spaces, zoning 46–8, 49

painting and decorating 63–88, 91, 120
   bathrooms 178
   colour-matched paint 76
   and environmental issues 195
   equipment 65
   expensive paint 76–7
   furniture 116
   half-painted walls 85–6
   and renters/first-time buyers 193
   tester pots 78–9
   tiles 67, 192
   types of paint 66–7
parquet 58
partners 38–9
patterns 71
Pebbles, Lily 91
percale 188–9
pets 54
picture rails 84
pictures 42, 168–9, 172, 193
Pike, Tom 59
pine 116
Pinterest 36, 37
pollution, particulate 108
primers 65, 67, 68, 69
purpose of a room 32–3

radiators 24, 41, 59, 67, 81, 95, 107, 139
'red thread' concept 114–15

renters 191–3
resin 139, 140, 180
restaurants 34
Robinson, Sophie 70
Rogers, E.M. 9
rolled steel joists (RSJs) 31
room dividers 45
rugs 46–7, 49–50, 61, 71, 112, 120, 192

Saarinen, Eero 143
sateen 188–9
Schoenauer, Norbert 46
shabby-chic 7, 116
shelving 51, 83, 106, 115
   bathroom 51, 177
   kitchen 146–7, 148
   landing 52
   living room 167
   open 47–8
   standard measurements 102
Shillingford, Marianne 38
shopping 18–19
'shopping your home' 30
showers 102, 178, 179–82
shutters 98
skirting boards 41, 81
skylights 52
Sloan, Annie 116
small spaces 41–4
social media 9
sockets 136
sofas 10–11, 19, 41, 43–4, 105, 111, 115, 120, 161–2
space dividers 46–8
special offers 18–19
splashbacks 151
spray paint 69
stain removal 55
stainless steel 140
stairs 54, 59–60, 66, 70, 102

standard measurements 102, 194
starting out 29–30
storage 51–2
    bathroom 51, 177, 180
    built-in 17, 20
    children's 62
    kitchens 51, 102, 146–8, 148, 151, 193–4
    living room 167
    see also cupboards; wardrobes
structural engineers 31
style, knowing your 6–7, 11
sustainability 10–11, 118, 187, 188
symmetry 37

tables 45, 112
bedside 186
coffee 41–2, 114, 163
dining/kitchen 17, 32, 45, 118, 133, 143
lighting 133
nested 163
taps 149, 178
televisions 164, 167
thread count 188–9

throwaway culture 10
tiles 18, 19, 192
    bathroom 178
    floor 139
    kitchen 151
    painting 67, 192
    work surface 141
toilets 34, 91, 182
towel rails, heated 180
toys 61
tradespeople 21, 25, 36, 40
trends 7, 8–11, 153
tungsten bulbs 123, 124, 125

underfloor heating 57, 59–60, 139, 180
underlay 54
upcycling 118, 193

velvet 39, 92, 162
vintage 118, 120
vinyl 56, 58
voile 98

wallpaper 24, 82, 87–8, 192
walls 24
    decorating 29, 65–7, 88

feature 83–4
    preparation 65, 88
    removal 24, 31
Ward, Chris 187
wardrobes 42
    walk-in/through 33, 183–4
watts 125
Who, What, When, Where, Why and How? method 12–21, 26
window dressings 42, 92–5, 97–8, 193
window film 98
windows 24, 68, 80, 89–102
wood
    engineered 57, 139
    flooring 57, 58, 112
    mixing 112, 114
    work surfaces 140
    wood-burning stoves 108–9, 193
woodwork 41, 66–7, 81, 120
wool 53, 54
work surfaces 140–1, 154

zoning 46–8, 49, 84

FEATURED PRODUCTS

Command™ strips (see Q91 and pages 172 and 193)
Dulux Easycare paint range (see Q25)
FrogTape® (see Q39)
PlastiKote® (see Q26)
Ronseal® DiamondHard Floor Paint (see Q25)
Ronseal® One Coat All Surface Primer and Undercoat (see Q26)
Rust-Oleum® (see Q27)
Zinsser AllCoat® Exterior (see Q26)
Zinsser B-I-N® (see Q24)

ACKNOWLEDGEMENTS

Huge thanks must go, as ever, to my agent, Jane Turnbull, who puts up with my endless questions on the arcane world of book publishing: Who has bought it? What do I need to do that for? But when will you know the answer? Where is that information? How do I get it? Perhaps now she has seen the format of this book, she will understand how my brain works.

Grateful thanks too, to all at Pavilion who worked so hard to make this book the perfect companion to the first and to realise my vision; my editors Steph and Krissy, publishing director Katie and designer Laura.

Special thanks to Abi Read, without whose gorgeous illustrations, our continued reinvention of the coffee table book would not be possible.

I love the colour of this book and it reminds me of the tiles at Russell Square station near the Pavilion office, which perhaps subliminally influenced my choice. I would also like to thank David Nicholls, the deputy editor of *House & Garden* (UK) who solved the conundrum of the title, which went on for ages.

But none of these thank yous would be necessary if it wasn't for you, my wonderful readers, who have endlessly supported the blog since its inception in 2012 (that's like ten decades in internet years) and whose constant questions form the basis for this second book. I appreciate every single one of your questions – even when you are just asking when Enid Cat will open her own Instagram account.

And from my online friends to my flesh and blood ones. To Hannah, without whom the gym would be much less fun, although potentially more productive. Tania, I will always talk paint colours and design with you and Caron, I miss you now that you have to work on Mondays. Cherry, we must have dinner more often.

Then there are those friendships that began virtually and are now IRL (as they say). So thank you to Bianca Hall, Lisa Dawson, Karen Knox, Kimberly Duran and Tania Quirk, all of who have contributed their wisdom to these pages.

And of course, to my friend, podcasting co-host and chief laughter correspondent, Sophie Robinson, who is a font of knowledge and joy along with our producer Kate Taylor, who knows how to manage us when we get too rowdy.

And finally, I wrote this at the end of the last book, aka Volume I, but it bears repeating as I'm not sure anything has changed much over the last couple of years. This book, as the last one did, must acknowledge all those who have no homes to frame their story. As in many major cities, London provides a constant reminder of the gap between homeowners and the homeless. For the last two years I have maintained a monthly donation to a homeless charity to try and do a tiny bit to redress the balance and to remind me to be grateful for what I have. Perhaps someone who reads this book might be willing to give something to the homeless charity of their choice too, in the hope that someone somewhere may also be given the chance of a home of their own.

MORE MAD ABOUT THE HOUSE

Find even more ideas and interiors inspiration in my first book, *Mad About the House: How to decorate your home with style*

Follow me on Instagram @mad_about_the_house

Keep up with the blog at www.madaboutthehouse.com

...AND THE PERFECT PODCAST

The Great Indoors is a celebration of all things interiors. In each episode, I discuss, debate and guide you through the top trends and hottest topics from the home front alongside co-host Sophie Robinson.